FINANCIAL WELLNESS FACTORS

Your path towards gaining control
of your money and your life

Gina Colalillo and Joseph Trombetta

One Printers Way
Altona, MB R0G 0B0
Canada

www.friesenpress.com

Copyright © 2023 by Gina Colalillo and Joseph Trombetta
First Edition — 2023

All rights reserved.

No part may be reproduced in any form, or by any means, including photocopying without permission in writing from Gina and Joseph.

Limit of Liability/Disclaimer of Warranty: While the authors have used their best efforts in preparing this book, they make no representation or warranties with respect to the accuracy of the contents of this book. The advice and strategies contained herein may not be suitable for your situation. Consult with a professional where appropriate. Authors shall not be liable for any loss of profit or consequential damages.

No part of this publication may be reproduced in any form, or by any means, electronic or mechanical, including photocopying, recording, or any information browsing, storage, or retrieval system, without permission in writing from FriesenPress.

ISBN
978-1-03-915647-0 (Hardcover)
978-1-03-915646-3 (Paperback)
978-1-03-915648-7 (eBook)

1. BUSINESS & ECONOMICS, PERSONAL FINANCE, MONEY MANAGEMENT

Distributed to the trade by The Ingram Book Company

FINANCIAL WELLNESS FACTORS

TABLE OF CONTENTS

FOREWORD	V
JOE	1
GINA	11
CASH FLOW	21
ATTITUDE	41
RELATIONSHIPS	57
HEALTH	71
BALANCE	87
NOW WHAT	97
AFTERWORD	101
ABOUT THE AUTHORS	105
ACKNOWLEDGMENTS	107

FOREWORD

It's been ten years since we originally wrote this book. Ten years! A lot has changed since then. When we first began writing this book back in 2012, we were on a mission to teach our (then much younger) sons about finance and balancing life. We really wanted this book to be a more holistic approach to finance; an overall financial wellness guide that ranged from controlling your money more effectively to creating financial stability and security for the future. But there was a very important reason that we wanted to write this book. A reason that goes over and above just sharing sound financial advice. And that reason was the thyroid cancer diagnosis that we got hit with in 2012. We were worried about the boys not having their father around and wanted to leave them with something, should treatment fail. So, these lessons and stories were important to capture and important enough for us to want to impart on our sons. With the weight of cancer treatment, managing our family, processing our emotions and running our business bearing down on us; the time for publishing the book just wasn't right.

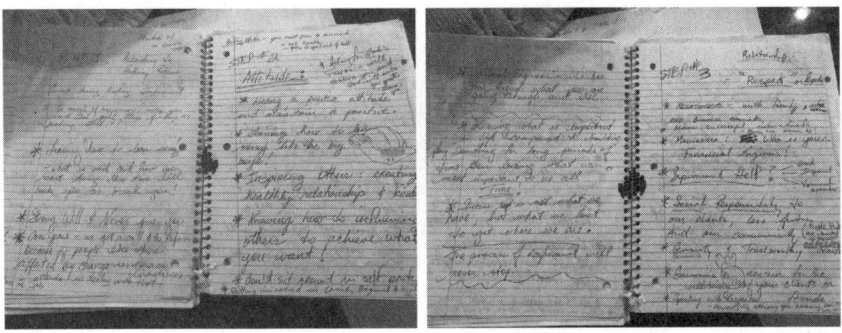

Notebook pages with thoughts, planning and ideas for the book. These pages represent the early days when *The Financial Wellness Factors* was first conceived.

A lot of good has happened in these past ten years. The main one is that we are both still here, healthier and happier than ever. We are grateful for that every single day. All our kids have now graduated post-secondary education and joined the family business, which we couldn't be happier about. Our eldest son, Daniel, is a mortgage agent and leads mortgage originations with his brother Matthew, our youngest, who is a finance specialist. Thomas, our middle son, assists us in asset management with a property management company that he heads up with our portfolio investment properties. Daniel also got married and had three beautiful daughters – Isabella, Valentina, and Natalia – with our beautiful daughter-in-law, Nicole. They bring joy and happiness to our whole family and have been such a blessing. We have also grown our mortgage lending company and the mortgage origination company, and now have twelve employees working with us. We are constructing a new office down the street from our current office, since we ran out of space and still need to hire more employees. We have evolved quite a bit over the last ten years. We are still assisting people in creating wealth preservation and creation strategies, from homeowners to investors. The best part is that we get to do this each and every day with our family, together, and that is truly a blessing.

In 2020, one of the most impactful, challenging, and catastrophic global events happened in more than a century – the COVID-19 pandemic. We went from "two weeks to flatten the curve" to endless weeks and months of lockdowns, quarantines, and companies having to completely rethink and reconfigure their operations and workforces. Companies big and small (ours included) had to figure out how to keep business running normally, with everyone at home. People were personally struggling, whether with fear of getting sick, actually being sick, or simply the isolation and loneliness of being away from friends, families, and communities. It was such a challenging time for our world. During lockdowns, we turned our attention to our family farm. We focused on special projects that improved the farm; everything from growing vegetables, to planting trees and reviving old grapevines. Having the farm really helped our mental health during the worst days of the pandemic. We also had the pleasure of spending more time with our beautiful granddaughters. The farm, our family, and our focus on togetherness was the best medicine we could have asked for during that time, as the world tried to find a cure and worked on vaccines and people argued relentlessly about beliefs and ideologies. We were obliviously happy in our little family bubble on our farm, focused on the things that we did have control over.

The interesting thing was coming back to Financial Wellness Factors after ten years, healing from cancer, a pandemic, our children becoming adults, expanding our business, and a war to discover that while much had changed in our lives, the advice we share in this book is constant and remains unchanged. It still holds true, even more so now than ever. With inflation causing significant strain on families affecting everything from mortgage payments to the cost of goods, food, hydro, gas, and more, now is the time to take action on your finances and take stock of your life to find out where you can improve. The pandemic and inflation actually created a sense of urgency for us to get this book out there. We knew it was more important now to finally publish and share this book with the world, since it can help so many. The factors have not changed since we first wrote the book.

We hope that you take comfort in knowing this, as we have, and that the lessons in this book will lead you on a path to wellness in every aspect of your life, including your finances.

Gina & Joe

JOE

We always tell our clients to prepare for the unexpected in life. God knows Gina and I have struggled with unexpected events throughout the duration of our marriage. We have been tried, tested, and put through the ringer, but it is also what makes us such a strong couple. We were neighbours when we met. Gina had just graduated from university and I had just started college. We hit it off right away, even though we were at different stages of our lives. We had a lot in common. It was four years after that that she married me – Joe Trombetta. I felt like the luckiest man on earth.

After our second boy, Nicholas, was born, he was diagnosed, at six weeks, old with a rare blood disorder called Langerhan Cell Histiocytosis. I remember the day that we were sitting at McMaster Children's Hospital in Hamilton as though it were yesterday. I still vividly remember the doctor's name and her telling us, "Your son is not going to live past the age of three." It felt like someone had shot me in the heart. How could we have ever thought of or anticipated that? We were both stunned and distraught beyond belief. There is just nothing you can do to prepare yourself for something like that. But eventually, after a great deal of grief, you have to move past it and be there to support the rest of your family. At the time, Daniel was four and Thomas was six months old. They needed us to be present. You don't ever get over a tragic event like this, but you have to keep moving forward. Our angel Nicholas was two and a half years old when he passed away. Two years later, Matthew was born.

left to right, Thomas, Nicholas, and Daniel

No matter what happens, you have a responsibility to your family to be there for them and support them through the ups and downs of life. You never really get over it when your child dies, but you simply must go on. You can't give up on life. After we had lost Nicholas and before we had our fourth child, I remember noticing a void within Gina. Financially. we were doing fine – we were both working full time with good jobs – but we were losing Gina somewhere, something was missing. Then, out of the blue, she became pregnant again, and Matthew was born. He has always been a special boy. He showed up at exactly the right time. Matthew realigned Gina. Of course, he could never replace Nicholas, but he helped heal her through the pain with his light and presence, and he completed the picture of our family.

Just as you cannot anticipate tragic events within your family, you also cannot always anticipate devastating financial loss or hardship. I started my own business in 1999 when Matthew was born. I started working toward the goal of accumulating wealth in the way that I knew, which was creating cash flow. At the time, I had started an investment arm in my business, and had a partner who propelled my wealth significantly. He had a lot of money invested in the business. Together, we met another businessman who needed money for a construction project, and of course, we were in the lending business. In order to borrow from us, he fed us exactly what we wanted to hear. He played into our greed by telling us that we would receive huge rates of return, beyond reason and logic. My partner and I unfortunately fell victim to this greed, and we went on to do the deal and lost everything. It was my first encounter with a financial sociopath. I would go on to meet many more people like this, which gave me the skills to recognize the signs and characteristics and avert any negative financial repercussions. Thankfully, the other side of my business (the mortgage business) was fine. But I had completely lost 80 percent of my savings on that one transaction with that one person. It was devastating. I looked at all of the people that were affected, either directly or indirectly, from the actions of this individual. It affected a great deal of people and made me feel awful. These were workers in the skilled trades who had worked on the construction site and completed the work, but then hadn't been paid for their work. These tradespeople couldn't make a mortgage payment after this happened, and they were coming to me for help. It was a very disappointing time in my life but could never compare to the tragedy we had already been through with the passing of our son.

I remember coming home, and I was so depressed over this stupid thing that I had caused. I was really depressed because the financial loss was greater than any amount of money I had or could access. And on top of that, I had to continue to pay lawyers. I felt that there was a strong possibility I would run out of cash. I worried about having enough money to meet my financial obligations.

Having gone through some difficult situations, I began thinking about my parents and their struggle as new immigrants to the country. When I think about how and why my parents immigrated to Canada, their story is really about *willingness*. This story is all too well known to all who have immigrated to Canada in search of a better life: the willingness to work hard, to be honest and respectful to others, and to learn the Canadian way no matter how many hurdles you face.

The single most important thing for any newcomer to Canada is to purchase a home to create your wealth and stability for your family. When my parents first arrived in Canada, they arrived on a boat that landed in Halifax. They were greeted by the Salvation Army, where my older sister was changed into a new outfit. They fed my parents and sister and got them to the train station. From Halifax, they traveled to Hamilton by train and arrived at what we know today as Liuna station. Sidenote: there's a beautiful painting by Joseph Mancinelli that beautifully captures a rare glimpse of the immigrants that would have passed through Liuna station during that time period.

My father's cousin came to pick my parents and sister up from Liuna Station and brought them back home to his house. Luigi quickly jumped into action by finding my father a job within days of first arriving- securing a blue collar job making an honest living at a local steel factory. Within nine months, my father purchased his first home on Cedar Avenue, close to Gage Park. During that same time, he sponsored my grandmother and grandfather on my mom's side (Emidio and Carmela D'Orazio). Wanting to show respect to my grandparents, the home on Cedar Avenue in Hamilton became their home. And within nine months, they purchased a home on Spadina Avenue, not far from my grandparents. Keep in mind, the average hourly rate was a dollar. Every dollar went to pay off that house debt. That story is all about the willingness to succeed for the family.

When you look at it from where I stand today, we, too, can grow financially and personally, just like our immigrant parents did. We need to break free from the shell of complacency and get out of our comfort zone.

During my time of financial turmoil, I decided to go and speak to my father. My parents knew that I was an up-and-coming success at the time. They saw me as a thriving businessman who was closing deals and had plenty of money. So they were surprised to hear about the financial difficulties I was going through as a result of the mortgage on the construction site. I had to pay my employees and cover the costs of my mortgage business. I said to my dad, *"I don't need help today, but in a couple of months, if things don't change for me drastically, I need a small loan. I am going to need $10 or $20K."*

The Early Days 1970, Cesidio and Maria Trombetta, Donna and Joseph (me) and baby Carmela

He said, *"I don't believe you. YOU need money? Get out of here."* But when he connected with me eye to eye, he realized that I wasn't kidding, and that I was in fact hurting. He turned around and said, *"OK. Don't worry about it. I got it."* Then, he asked my mom to bring him the chequebook.

I never did take the cheque that day, but I wanted and needed to know that my dad was behind me. I started thinking outside of the box. There was a piece of land that I knew about that could not be sold in its current use. I didn't know anything about investing in land or land assembly, but I had a hunch and followed it. I acquired additional lands to complete a parcel I could now sell, and with the housing market rebounding, I was able to make a profit. So, karma was balanced, in a sense. Yes, an individual took advantage of me, but I came back by taking a gamble during a desperate time. I doubled down and it worked out successfully for me. I won the court case against the guy who had taken advantage of me, and my business was growing in leaps in bounds. It was a positive change, and the jumpstart that I needed to change my life. I took those earnings and put them into another investment, which again made me double the amount of money – again in land development. I still, to this day, have a company in land development. You can't give up. Don't lose faith, ever.

In the end, weirdly, I was thankful for the lesson I received by being taken advantage of, even though it was a tough one. That mistake, that life lesson, I vowed, would never occur in my life again, or in my clients lives. I had learned and grown from the experience. I wouldn't let my guard down. I knew the feeling now, and I knew what to look for.

During that uncertain period of time, it was Gina who reminded me that we had already gone through the worst thing in life when we had lost our son, Nicholas. She helped to push me through and showed me that if I could survive and live through that, I could survive anything. This was a walk in the park compared to that. I wasn't planning on being screwed over in business and losing 80 percent of my savings, but it happened. And thanks to the support and love of my family, I made it out of that situation as a wiser, stronger, and more humbled man.

Life has a lot of curveballs. I realized the importance of being content with where you are in life at this moment and the importance of continuing to work toward your goals without feeling that you are unlucky, unsuccessful, or not quite there yet. There are things beyond our control, and you can guarantee that things will happen that we are not anticipating. When I was diagnosed with cancer in January of 2012, I wasn't planning on getting sick. I never saw that in my future, but it happened, and I dealt with it by managing it in the best way that I could. Nobody plans to get in an accident or plans to get sick. I realized that I should just be happy in the moment and be happy with what I have.

I have always been intrigued by what makes someone a success. From the time I first started out in business, I began really analyzing successful people to ascertain what traits contributed to their success. I evaluated each intriguing success story by criteria I developed in my mind – things that I thought made them successful. I examined these people based on things like their business philosophy, personality traits, and behaviours. This methodology of evaluating successful people developed over a number of years through my personal observation of others in business who I looked up to. When I was younger, I thought that being successful meant being wealthy and having lots of cash in the bank. I later realized that being successful meant so much more than that. The true success stories were the ones who were wealthy, philanthropic, caring, and honest; they had great relationships and families. I realized that it was much more than their commitment to earning that made them a success. In discovering this, I also had to be disappointed in finding out that some of the people I looked up to and thought were successful, in fact, were not.

There was one entrepreneur in particular who I remember just idolizing. He was *the man*. He appeared to have it all. I would look at him and think that I wanted to be like him. Everybody knew him or was connected to him in some way; he seemed to be wealthy and very connected, and it looked like he had the world in the palm of his hands. But it wasn't long before the veil of this illusion lifted, and I saw that his life in fact wasn't as successful as I wanted to believe. He had monetary success, but that was really all he had. He wasn't an honourable person, he wasn't generous or caring, and his personal relationships were falling apart. This really rocked me, because it made me rethink my criteria for evaluating successful people. I suddenly realized that it wasn't just about how much material wealth you had, but how you balance your life in all areas.

I realized that balance was key to long-lasting success. Financial stability was just one component of what made someone successful, but there were others that were equally important. Over the years, how I gauged success began changing. It wasn't all about financial stability anymore. As time went on and my views matured, I realized that there were more factors involved, and that's where the seed of this book began to sprout.

It was through this process of observation and discovery over a number of years that Gina and I developed a formula for success: The Factors of Financial Wellness. We often consulted our clients on much more than getting a mortgage and a home. We became their trusted financial advisors and lifestyle consultants, in a sense. We wanted to help them succeed in the long haul and give them all of the tools required – not just to have enough money when they needed it, but to be financially happy and healthy, so they could enjoy their success. Our clients sought our expertise, and we began teaching them The Factors, because The Factors became our philosophy and what we knew to be true. The Factors can be applied at any level. We know this because we have witnessed clients of varying financial levels experience great success by embracing The Factors' methodology. It doesn't matter how much money you have or don't have.

One might be wealthy but perhaps not successful in other areas of life, just as one might be broke financially but already possess most other attributes of what makes someone a success. Almost everyone can benefit in some way by learning The Factors and applying the best practices to their lives. Even if someone is already a financial success, The Factors can still serve as a checklist for life balance, to ensure that every area of life is in harmony. Just having millions of dollars squirreled away isn't enough. What are you doing to give back? Are you healthy and well balanced? Are you socially responsible? Are you emotionally healthy? These things are so important to financial wellness. Money is only one aspect of financial wellness. And what good is money without the ability to enjoy it and appreciate where it came from?

The hardest Factor for people to get is cash flow. And we can take an example from the financial crisis that happened in 2008 in the US to understand why. People just aren't living within their means. It sounds simple, but it's the hardest thing for people to grasp. They have a certain amount of cash flow coming in and they are living beyond it with no savings and barely enough to cover the bills. It's such a basic message, but it's such a common problem for a lot of our clients and other people who are struggling financially. We're not here to judge anybody. But if you want to attain financial wellness, you just have to live within your means. That's exactly why the financial collapse occurred in the United States. Banks were lending to anyone, and people were going out and buying houses based on being a waiter and earning $20K a year, buying a huge house because they had the credit to do it. You have to look at where you are now and deal with the reality of that before you can work to get to where you want to be.

One of the recommendations that I always talk about is maintaining a budget. Having a surplus at the end of the month is very important. Shoot for 10 percent or so. If you are living paycheque to paycheque, it's not a good morale builder. You are like a hamster on a wheel; you aren't going anywhere yet you are working hard to stay on the wheel. The budget is important. You have to have a pulse on your finances. You can't be detached from it, and simply ignoring it won't make it any better. Take an active role in your financial life to manage every penny you have. And when you do have money left over, think about what you do with it. Ideally, you want your surplus to be invested somewhere so that your capital makes capital. That might mean buying a franchise business, a rental property, or land. Your capital investment has to make capital. I buy people's private mortgages because it gives me an investment that provides cash flow.

Warren Buffett is a great example of how to invest. He would rather pay more money for a wonderful company than get a great deal on an OK company. Because chances are, the wonderful company is going to make him more money in the long run. You have to think about long-term cash flow and invest where it makes sense. At first you may not have a lot of money to play with, so the investments you choose will be important. Weigh all of your options and decide what makes the most sense for you.

Life is too short. We have to look at what's important in life. It's not about becoming a multi-millionaire. It's about doing the best you can with what you have in each moment of life while working toward your goals. If you're already wealthy, the message is, *what have you done for your community today*? You can provide more than the average person out there. So what are you doing today to improve the quality of life for your community and the world at large? But that message rings true for everyone – whether you have more money than you need or you hope to attain more. We can all get involved and do more within our community. How are you sharing your time? How are you getting involved? Giving back to your community? Creating *good* extends far beyond helping your community. It helps your soul and your well-being.

My hope for you is that in reading *The Financial Wellness Factors*, you will discover what areas of your life are in need of balance. Whether it's an increase in wealth you seek, stronger relationships, or just a healthier life, this book will help you balance your life in more ways than one. Remember, money is just one part of the equation.

Gina and I share our stories and experiences so that you can see that the path to our success hasn't been a linear one. We've faced obstacles, setbacks, tragedies, and unexpected events that have continually caused us to have to readjust our course and persevere. We didn't come from wealthy families who bankrolled our businesses and lives. We put the work in, from humble beginnings, and took some risks to get where we are today.

GINA

My first financial mentor was my father. He taught me the value of a dollar and would always tell me, *"It doesn't matter how much money you make, if you can't save money then you'll never be able to build a financially stable life."* I have always taken that advice to heart.

My story is no different than many immigrant families who arrived in Canada in search of a better life with greater opportunity. My parents actually immigrated to Australia first. They got married, bought a home, and were building a good life for themselves. At the time, my father's family was spread between Italy, Australia, and Canada, and they had a vision of reuniting in one country and working together to become more successful. The goal was to keep the family together. My parents immigrated to Canada in 1961. The vision of having all the family together, sadly, didn't work as planned, and my father ended up with two sisters in Italy, a sister and brother in Australia, and four brothers in Canada, as everyone settled where they were.

When my parents arrived in Canada, they knew the importance of purchasing land to gain some stability for the family. They were farmers in Italy, and having land was very important to them to produce income. One of the properties they purchased in 1965 was in Stoney Creek; a ten-acre farm with grapes and cherries (the same property we now live at with our family). Back then, my family and I lived in a small, 700-square-foot, two-bedroom farmhouse for a couple of years with my uncle and his family. There were eight of us in total living in that tiny home. I still have fond memories of that time and that house. The house never felt small to me as a child. It's only now that I think back on those days that I wonder how we managed with everyone together in such a small space.

Mom and Dad sitting in front of their first house in Australia, 1959

Our Family Farm in 1967, 8 of us lived in the farmhouse which is now our current residence lot, left to right, my Dad, me, my sister, and two cousins

Eventually, in 1969, we moved into the east end of Hamilton. Both my parents had factory jobs. They would work shifts, and a lot of responsibility fell on my sister and I from quite a young age. My parents not only had their full-time factory jobs, but they also had the farm to manage as well. My father and his brother purchased the farm together, and our family would farm after school and on weekends. We produced concord grapes, which we sold to Winona Gardens (owned by George Smith at the time). We'd pick cherries and sell them to E. D. Smith, or simply set up a farm stand by the side of the road to sell to passing vehicles. We were all involved in the success of our family's farm, and everyone had a role to play.

These were years that I'd never forget. We worked together as a family to build our wealth, and my parents did the best they could without an education. These years are where I say I developed my strong work ethic, working long hours, never complaining and never expecting anything in return, such as an allowance – there was no such thing at that time! We lived within our means and always saved for the future. My parents worked the farm for as long as possible, but when my sisters, cousins, and I all went off to university, there was no one left to assist them on the farm.

left to right, Gina, Antonio (Dad), Maria (sister), Santa (Mom), and Lea (sister), 2019

My parents encouraged my sisters and I to go to university. They saw it as an important way for their daughters to build independence and be financially well off. I went to university in 1982 and started in general business. After the first year, I made the decision to switch to a computer science and economics program, not because I loved it, but because I knew I could find a job in this rapidly emerging field. After graduating, in 1986, I immediately found a job at Shell in Toronto, earning $24,000 as a computer programmer. Shell was a great company to work at. They had already identified women as a minority and were working toward placing more women in senior management roles, which I saw as very progressive. If I had stayed, I know I could have done well there and moved up the ranks. But I wanted to be back in Hamilton, so I took a job at Stelco.

I met Joe in 1986, when our parents moved into the same subdivision and we became neighbours. Joe was younger than I was, and at the time, that made a big difference. I was working full time, and Joe was just starting college. I always thought Joe was very mature for his age. He had been working since he was twelve years old with his father in construction, and already owned his own company. We had a lot in common – the same family values and religious beliefs, strong worth ethic, and tons of ambition. It was inevitable that we'd end up together.

We married in 1990, and purchased our first home for $158,000. It was a four-level, backsplit and fairly new. Two of the levels were not finished. We knew that if we put in some sweat equity into the home, we could sell it later for a higher price. We were both working at the time. Though rates were over 7 percent, we chose not to over-extend ourselves. We had enough money to do the renovations. We lived there for a couple of years. However, when it came time to sell, the economy was in a recession, so nothing was selling at the time. Our home sat on the market for months with no activity, and we had already committed ourselves to another house purchase. It was a stressful situation to be in. We found an interested buyer who had a great income – and bad credit, but a decent down payment. So we decided to set up a rent-to-own deal with him and were able to sell the house for the purchase price at fair market value. This was our first creative financing deal that we put together, and it worked out well for us.

Our first boy, Daniel, was born in 1992, followed, a few years later, by Nicholas. All went well with the pregnancy, but after Nicholas was born, I started noticing a consistent diaper rash when he was about two months old – which I thought was strange, since I was nursing him. It was painful for him, and started to spread. He was healthy otherwise, eating well and in the ninetieth percentile for his age. But a dermatologist diagnosed him at the age of two months with a very rare disorder known as Langerhan Cell Histiocytosis. It was considered to be an orphan disease, and not much information was known about it at the time. This diagnosis would take us on a rollercoaster of stress and emotion for two years. We were in and out of the hospital, dealing with constant infections, chemotherapy treatment and surgeries, traveling to the US to speak to top doctors who had treated this condition to obtain more information and learn about other treatment options.

Nicholas absolutely loved Barney, and one of our highlights with him during this time was when Joe contacted the group in Texas that produced the Barney show and they actually arranged to have the real Barney come to the McMaster Children's hospital. We had to keep this quiet, since the popularity of this show was at an all-time high, and the hospital didn't want crowds of people showing up with their kids to catch a glimpse of the beloved dino.

Nicholas was in a lot of pain at the time, but he was so happy to see Barney, and I'll never forget that joy in his face. We had a parade in ward 3C, and they brought toys for everyone. To this day, whenever I run into a nurse or doctor that worked in that ward during that time, they always tell me how much it meant to them to be part of that with us.

Nicholas (1996)

While we were going through all of this with Nicholas, we found out I was pregnant again. We had Thomas. We didn't expect it, but it was an absolute blessing. Thomas was such an easygoing baby. Looking back, I don't really know how we managed this with everything going on in our lives – the back-and-forth to the hospital and the stress of a very sick child. But somehow, we managed. Daniel was four and Thomas was six months old when Nicholas passed away. It was the worst time in our lives. A part of me died with him that day – February 17, 1997. Words cannot describe the pain I went through. It was agonizing. But I had a newborn child and a four-year-old who needed their mom, and I had to be strong for them. As time moved on and we began to heal from the tragedy of Nicholas's passing, we went on to have another child, Matthew, our youngest son and another absolute blessing in our lives.

left to right, Thomas, Matthew and Daniel (2003)

In 1999, Joe decided that he wanted to start his own business working as a mortgage agent for a local mortgage brokerage. By this time, we had paid off our mortgage and with my stable job with a steady income, we had enough cash flow and savings set aside. I knew he wasn't happy in his career. Although his career was flourishing and he had the honour of being a top mortgage producer for the bank, something was missing. He wanted to accomplish more with his career and work on his own terms. I saw this entrepreneurial spirit in him and reassured him that my income was enough to support our family and that I wholeheartedly supported him starting a business. This meant a lot of extra hours and time spent away from home, away from me, and away from our young boys. At the time, Joe was working with another seasoned investor, and they were funding a new construction project. At some point, I knew things weren't going well with that endeavour. The project was running out of money, and so were we. I tried to reassure him that we would figure out a way to complete the project and get through it the best we could. We had already been through the hardest loss in our life, and losing money didn't compare to that. We were young and motivated and could start again.

During this time, I felt Joe was out of balance. He was working long hours, stressed over our financial picture, raising a young family. I was concerned about his mental and physical health. I knew that the negative effects of stress could lead to severe health consequences and wanted to combat those effects before they manifested physically. I came up with a plan for us to exercise together regularly, and that's what we put into place. Despite our busy schedules, we pushed each other, and have always made this a priority in our lives. This has helped us tremendously, both mentally and physically. Taking control of your health is essential, because at the end of the day, your health is your wealth. Nutrition and exercise have always been an essential part of who I am. Spending time making healthy meals for my family makes me happy and contributes to my overall well-being in a big way.

In 2002, I decided that I needed a change. My life was now out of balance. We had three boys, all involved in multiple sports, Joe was working toward building his business, and I was just not happy. It was a difficult decision to leave my job, but I knew that's what I had to do. I thought when I took the position that I would be there until I retired. After all, it offered me great money and benefits. But with more work hours and the possibility of having to move to Toronto, I decided it was time for me to make a move. I had supported Joe when he had to make a move, and now, it was my turn.

I went to Brock University and enrolled in a teachers' program. After graduating, I worked in the summer a few hours a week to assist Joe with his business. I never applied for a teaching position, because in helping Joe part time, I realized that I could be a valuable asset with my skill set, and help out the business. When I suggested this to Joe, he was unsure, and had so many questions. How would we work together? How would this affect our relationship and our family? I didn't give Joe much of a choice, as I recall, but in retrospect, it was the best decision I ever made. It wasn't always easy to work together, and still isn't some days, but I feel it gave us the work-life balance we both needed. We have more time to spend together in some way or another. We completely understand each other and often unload our complaints and challenges onto each other. It is actually really nice to work with your partner, knowing they will always have your back. We both understand our strengths and use them to the benefit of our clients. I believe the key is to both communicate and respect each other's professional roles, maintain boundaries, and leave work-related conflicts at the workplace. That's the only way to successfully navigate working with your partner. We are very lucky to have built this business successfully and created meaningful wealth for our family, together by each other's side, while also raising our family.

In 2012, our world came crashing down when Joe was diagnosed with thyroid cancer. It was another massive hurdle that our family had to overcome. This was a period of great reflection for Joe. He spent a lot of time looking back on his career and decisions he had made, and began writing things down. He wanted to share his life and experiences, and leave something behind for our kids and loved ones, should the unthinkable happen. Although Joe was in treatment, none of us truly knew if he would be OK and whether the treatment would be effective. So, we had to cherish each and every day we shared together. Joe started recalling stories from his past – lessons and crucial financial advice. These notes eventually evolved into Financial Wellness Factors. These are the lessons that he wanted to impart on our children – the lessons that we have lived together – and I know they will help you, too.

CASH FLOW

Cash flow is the most difficult aspect of personal finance for people to grasp and put into practice. It is a very simple concept in theory, but it is challenging for people to practice because it almost always requires some kind of undesired or disciplined behavioural change. We get comfortable with our lives; we enjoy spending, having credit cards available, and not having to worry about money. But if we are doing all of that while we have mounting credit debt and little savings in the bank, we are kidding ourselves. The only way to achieve financial comfort (without relying heavily on money we don't have) is to manage the money that we do have effectively. If we live month-to-month with no concept of what it costs to run the house, pay the bills, and how much is left over at the end of that, we are destined for failure and will get stuck in a cycle of negativity with money – never quite having enough and always being in a state of lack rather than abundance.

Managing your cash flow doesn't have to mean eating ramen noodles and giving up your social life; a few simple adjustments to the way you are currently living can make a big difference to your family finances. In this section, we will discuss what some of those things are and how you can make some modifications to your family finances so that you can be on your way to financial wellness without having to become somebody that you're not. When we work with clients, our goal is always to look at how they live, what is important to them, and what makes them happy, so that we can account for that within their budget. If you take away everything that you love, much like the nutritional diet, the financial diet may fail you. But if you build in allowances for rewards and luxuries here and there, you are more likely to succeed at managing your money and won't feel like you are sacrificing your entire way of life to reach your financial goals.

WHAT IS CASH FLOW?

Simply put, cash flow is the money that comes in and goes out. In the case of your family finances, it is very important to know what your monthly expenses are versus your income. In order to have positive cash flow and live within your means, you must bring in more than you pay out. Sound simple? It is, but unfortunately, it's the part that we all struggle most with. Why? Because as a society, we just love to spend money that we don't have. We rack up credit card debt, take out loans against our homes, and end up running on the hamster wheel of life every month to try to make payments for things that keep our debt load high and deplete our actual income. So, by the time we pay everybody that we owe money to, we are left with very little, or sometimes nothing at all, causing us to live on credit to buy everyday things like groceries, necessities, or clothing. This is a bad place to be.

One of the most important things we teach when working with clients is that the lifestyle has to meet the current debt load. If you are living like a rock star but only making minimum payments, it is going to take you decades to pay off your debt, and you are never truly going to get ahead. You'll always be crunched for cash. So in order for us to help, we ask all of our clients to take a realistic look at lifestyle and debt load to make sure that they are living within their means while making adequate payments on their debt load.

WHY IS CASH FLOW IMPORTANT?

Cash flow is important because it's the only way for you to get ahead of your finances. If you have no concept of what is coming in and going out, you will be unable to manage your money in a way that will lead you to financial security. You will be perpetually running on the hamster wheel, trying to make payments and catch up, and struggling to get by while living paycheque to paycheque. When you know and understand what your monthly expenses are and know what you have coming in each month, you can create a budget that allows you some room to make payments, have a bit of spending money, and put some aside for savings. Knowing what your cash flow looks like is the first and most important step to obtaining financial wellness. Sometimes, we close our eyes and think, "If I don't know how bad it is, maybe it will get better." Well, the opposite, in fact, is true. When we close our eyes and hope our financial difficulties will just go away, they in fact become more challenging and even more out of control. There really is no getting around this stage.

We can't push the responsibility off on someone else, pretend the debt is not there, hope it gets better, or ignore budgeting all together. If financial wellness is a goal of yours, and you want to be in a position of financial security, you are going to have to get comfortable with looking at the figures each month and taking an active role in managing your money. If it is a stressful affair for you, with regular practice, you will become somewhat desensitized to it and will look at it with a more practical set of eyes. It is only stressful when we come at it from a place of fear. There is nothing to fear about being in control of our finances.

CREATING A BUDGET

This is the part that scares everyone. The word *budget* makes people cringe for some reason. But really it should make you excited, because sticking to a budget will help you amass wealth and savings. Creating a budget is essential to your family's financial success. It is not enough to just know how much you have coming in and going out each month; you have to put something down on paper and ensure that the family sticks to the plan. Creating a chart with your income, expenses, and savings is the easiest way to do this, and you can use paper, a whiteboard, or even your computer to create a spreadsheet. How you create the chart isn't as important as how you use it. Make sure that wherever you create it, it is somewhere accessible, so that you can refer to it regularly and make adjustments when necessary.

When you set aside money for things and you overspend what you allocated, make sure you add what you actually spent to your budget so that you can readjust. This will also help you to identify where you are overspending, or perhaps where you need to increase your budget if you have not allocated enough to specific areas. A budget is a living, breathing document, and should never just be left once created. It will evolve daily as your spending, expenses, and financial emergencies occur.

Some people prefer to use software programs for their budgeting, others use an Excel spreadsheet, or some prefer to use paper or a whiteboard. Use whichever method you are the most comfortable using, regardless of what anyone tells you. The point with your budget chart is that you get comfortable with it, refer to it often, and continually use it and adjust it. Start by calculating your gross annual income (total amount the household brings in) and the monthly net income (how much you have each month). Then, begin tracking all of your fixed monthly expenses based on what you paid out the preceding month. Your fixed expenses are expenses that occur each month. They may vary slightly in amount based on usage in some instances, or they may be the same month to month. The fixed expenses are the ones that you have to pay every month, no matter what.

Some examples of fixed monthly expenses are mortgages or leases, car insurance, car payments, childcare expenses, loans, cell phone bills, Internet, hydro, etc. We think you get the idea. Since some bills change slightly month to month, let's base this budget on what you spent last month. Create a line item in your budget for each monthly expense that you have. Also, chart what you spend each month on other items, like entertainment, eating out, travel, clothes, etc. This is most likely the part that is going to require some changing, but for now, chart it by analyzing what you spent on these things last month.

Once you have charted your income, your fixed expenses, and what you spent on other things like groceries, food, gas, and entertainment, calculate how much you brought in versus how much you paid out. What is the difference in the dollar amount? If you brought in $6,000 last month and spent all of it without any left in savings, there is a problem. Similarly, if you spent most of it, with only a hundred or two left for emergencies, you also need some adjusting. Typically, it is recommended that you save about 10 percent of your gross monthly income each month to put towards your savings. This, in addition to following your budget, is how you will begin to build your nest egg. To calculate what 10 percent of your gross monthly income would be, simply add up all of your monthly income sources, divide them by 100, and then multiply that by 10. For example, if your gross monthly income is $6,000, once you divide that by 100, you are left with 60; multiply that by 10 and you arrive at 600. This means that based on a gross monthly income of $6,000, you should be setting aside $600 each month for savings.

Now that you know how to calculate your savings, take a look at your expenses and your budget. Where are you overspending? Are you eating out three or four times a week? Are you buying your lunch every day instead of bringing it to work? Do you spend a lot on clothing and entertainment? Remember, you are basing this on what you spent last month as a way to move forward with your budget. Now that you know what your monthly household income is, what your expenses are, and how much you need to save each month, you can look at your budget and adjust it accordingly.

Some expenses you will not be able to cut back on, such as loans and other fixed expenses. But if you are spending too much in one particular area and can scale back (listen to your intuition, you will know), then that is the area you should focus on first.

You are going to have to get honest with yourself during this process and really think about wants versus needs. Of course, you can continue to spend the way you are and continue living as you are without sacrifice, but you will never get ahead if you do, and you could find yourself in a serious financial crisis. You wouldn't be reading this book if you didn't already feel the need to make changes to your financial life. We are experts at helping people manage their money and budget for financial success. You may experience some short-term pain for long-term gain throughout this process, but it will be well worth it in the end when you see the savings in your bank account.

The majority of people who face financial hardship are overspending. So, the first thing you must do is *stop* spending money you don't have by continuing to add debt to your credit cards. You will focus on paying these down, not using them as a source of money when you feel an impulse to buy something that you don't need. Your budget will help you uncover areas where you are overspending. Perhaps you have never really seen just how much you are spending in a particular area before, but you should take the time to calculate it and know what the numbers are. Even buying a coffee every day at a high-end coffee shop can add up to $100 per month. It is much more economical to make it yourself. Ask yourself, "Do I need to spend x amount on x each month, or do I just want to?" You will inherently know what your wants versus needs are.

Until you are on a roll, you're going to have to get tough with yourself and focus primarily on your needs. This means covering your basic necessities each month, paying your bills, and setting some aside for savings. You can allocate a small amount of money in your budget for entertainment and eating out, but this should be nominal, otherwise you will find yourself in the same predicament, with no money in savings, barely scraping by each month. It is very important that your lifestyle meets your current debt load.

Here's our lifestyle assessment tool that we frequently provide to our clients at Titan Mortgage to help them figure out what their monthly expenses are versus their disposable income. This budget plan is a crucial first step to effectively managing your cash flow. Feel free to go through this exercise yourself after reading this chapter by entering these figures into a spreadsheet or even just writing it out on paper. Sometimes the results are surprising, especially if this is unfamiliar territory for you.

Monthly Take Home Income	
Salary/Wages/Business Draw	
Salary or Wages (Spouse)	
Pension/Retirement	
Interest on Accounts	
Alimony / Child Support	
Real Estate rent (income)	
Investment Dividends	
Unemployment	
Other	
Total Take Home Income	

Monthly Living Expenses	
Alimony / Child Support (outgoing)	
Auto Gas and Repair	
Auto Insurance	
Cable TV/ Satellite Fees	
Charitable Contributions	
Child Care	
Childrens' Activities	
Clothing Maintenance (Laundy/Dry cleaning	
Clothing Purchases	
Electricity Bill	
Food (In-home / Groceries)	
Food (Out of home - Lunch, Dining)	
Health and Dental Insurance	
Homeowner/Condo fees	
Homeowners/ Renters Insurance	
Internet Access (AOL,MSN, DSL)	
Life and Disability Insurance	
Memberships (Health club etc.)	
Personal Care (Grooming)	
Prescriptions	
Property Services (Gardener,Pool)	
Security Services (Alarm)	
Subscriptions	
Telephone (Home, Cell, Pager)	
Trash Disposal	
Tuition and School Supplies	
Water Bill	
Property Insurance	
Property Tax	
Income Tax payment to CCRA	
Total Monthly Living Expenses	

Secured Debts (Monthly Payments)	
Rent	
1st Mortgage	
Land Lease (Trailer park, other)	
Student Loans	
Auto Loans/Leases	
Recreation (Boat, ATV, etc.)	
Past Due Taxes	
2nd Mortgage	
Other Debts	
Other Loans	
Other Loans	
Total Secured Debt	

Unsecured Debt	
Credit Card 1	
Credit Card 2	
Credit Card 3	
Credit Card 4	
Credit Card 5	
Credit Card 6	
Credit Card 7	
Credit Card 8	
Personal Loan 1	
Personal Loan 2	
Other	
Other	
Total unsecured Debt	

Summary	
Total Take Home (Income)	
Total Living Expenses (-)	
Total Secured Debt Payments (-)	
Total Unsecured Debt Payments (-)	
Disposable Income **	
Disposable Income as Percent	

A healthy budget will have 5-10% disposable income. If your calculations reveal a deficit (in parentheses) you may be in serious debt. We can help.

WHAT IS A BUDGET PLAN?

A budget plan is a chart that shows you the flow of money in your everyday life. A budget can help you determine where you are overspending as well as help you adjust bad spending habits. By making slight adjustments to your budget, you may have the ability to save more or make larger payments on your debts.

WHY DO I NEED A BUDGET PLAN?

Every day, thousands of consumers face financial crises. These can be caused by personal or family illness, or loss of a job, but the most common is overspending. By tracking your spending, you will know exactly where your money is going.

Our society encourages consumers to *buy now, pay later*, offering credit cards and convenience to spend more everywhere we look. This is why it is so easy to get carried away with spending, and eventually end up knee-deep in debt. A budget is designed to help consumers gain control of their spending, and with proper planning, it can help to improve your financial situation.

HOW TO CREATE A BUDGET PLAN

Start by keeping track of all your monthly living expenses and other monthly bills. There is a vast selection of budgeting software out there, but they all cost money. Creating a budget can be done by simply using a spreadsheet on a computer or recording on a piece of paper. We have provided a simple budget plan in this chapter. Should you have questions about it, please do not hesitate to contact us.

HOW DO I MAINTAIN MY BUDGET PLAN?

You need to control your emotions and impulses that stimulate your desire to spend money. You should keep close track of what you spend every day. Ask yourself, "Do I really need to buy this? Maybe I should bring my lunch instead of eating out." See where you can cut back on your fixed monthly expenses. But if that's difficult, you should always be able to cut back on your personal care, hobbies, and entertainment.

HOW TO PLAN FOR MILESTONES AND EMERGENCIES

There are many different types of financial emergencies that can strike when you least expect it. Losing a job, a death in the family, or purchasing a new car are all situations that can leave you with financial problems if they are not properly prepared for. It is recommended that you set aside at least six times your monthly living expenses to cover you in case of a major emergency.

CONSOLIDATION

Sometimes, we meet with clients whose expenses are greater than their income. They are up to their eyeballs in debt and unable to save any extra. This is a dangerous position to be in, and can ruin a family if a financial emergency crops us. Sometimes things – like illness, death, or car trouble – can cause significant financial hardship in the family. If your expenses exceed your income, and you have no money in savings and are living paycheque to paycheque, it is unlikely that you are going to be able to manage such a financial emergency with any degree of success. In fact, an event like that will ruin you if you have no surplus or access to funds in case of an emergency. And let's face it: life is unpredictable sometimes. We don't always know what is going to happen and when. We have been there ourselves, in the face of adversity, completely blindsided by events that we had no prior knowledge of. When expenses exceed income, it is very important to look at consolidating debt. If you are unfamiliar with this term, what it basically means is that you take out a loan to pay off all of your debts and then you pay that one debt off.

For example, if you are paying off your car, two credit cards, and a student loan, you would apply for a new loan in the amount of all of those debts. The new loan would be enough to pay each of those debts off, and once completed, you would simply have one loan to pay off instead of four. This helps you manage your interest and payments each month and stops you from forgetting dates or making late payments. The simpler your financial life, the easier it will be for you to manage. Remembering one payment is far easier than remembering seven. So for this reason, consolidation is a great idea. It is also important to look at which of your debts are tax deductible, because you can write certain things off when tax time rolls around. The ones that are not tax deductible should be eliminated first, as they are the ones that are not doing you any favours.

The goal with debt consolidation is to increase cash flow. For example, if your family income is $6,000 per month and your total amount of fixed monthly expenses comes to $5,000, it doesn't leave much wiggle room. But if you were to consolidate your debts and your new monthly payment is

$2,500, that leaves significantly more money each month to put towards savings and pay off additional debt. You could even increase the amount of the consolidation payment and pay off extra each month and still be in better shape than you were before you consolidated your loans. We are big advocates of debt consolidation because it is a great way to realize additional cash flow each month. If your expenses exceed your income, consolidation is a must for you. Even if your expenses do not exceed your income, but you have a lot of debts to pay off each month, you may still want to look at consolidation.

WHEN TO CONSOLIDATE

Here are some reasons to consider consolidating your debt:

- Your expenses exceed your income.
- You are struggling to make minimum payments.
- You have more than three or four credit card payments to make each month.
- You are just barely scraping by due to your credit payments.

CREATING RESIDUAL INCOME

When you manage your cash flow effectively and create a surplus at the end of each month by either consolidating your debt or simply sticking to your budget, you create the opportunity to invest your money resulting in residual income. You are taking the money that you have left over and investing it in a bond or portfolio that will yield you a return on your money. This means that your money will now begin to work for you by making you more money.

Here's how it works for us. We invest in private mortgages. When a customer comes to us and we cannot get the loan approved through the banking channel or an alternative lender, we lend them private money to finance their mortgage if it makes sense and is suitable for the client, and we are certain the client can afford this mortgage payment. Our capital is invested to make interest income from the private mortgage we have given to the customer. They will pay monthly and amortize over thirty years. Our capital will then make an income, which, in turn, we will lend to other customers that don't qualify for bank mortgages. This perpetual stream of income will continue to make more capital, which we continuously invest and reinvest back into our company.

You may not be ready for residual income yet if you are just beginning to budget and save, but it is something you should at least begin thinking about. Think about how you can create residual income for your family. What makes the most sense for you? Do you have any investments anywhere? Are you making interest on any of your money? Could you begin to? Creating a source of residual income is a major key to amassing wealth. Remember this as you are sticking to your budget and setting money aside each month. If you are building a nest egg in a savings account, why not get that money working for you, creating further capital for your family? It is something that you ought to begin thinking about now. Look for opportunities to invest in businesses or investments that yield a return on your money. Once you begin identifying these opportunities, further opportunities will present themselves to you.

JOE'S EARLY LESSON ON INFLATION

Inflation will always eat up all your money's purchasing power. I remember an early lesson on inflation when my grandfather, back in the early eighties, was teaching me how to negotiate purchasing a property.

I used to cut grass at my grandfather's house on Saturdays or Sundays when I wasn't working with my dad. There were two old ladies who lived beside my grandfather. When I cut my grandfather's property's grass, I would always cut theirs, too.

I never wanted anything in return. It was a gesture of goodwill on my part, without expectation. But in return, they would always prepare freshly squeezed lemonade and freshly baked cookies for me, which I always appreciated.

One day, after knowing the ladies for quite a while, they offered me the purchase of their home, with all their belongings and the Nova SS in the garage. They wanted $40,000 all in for everything. So, I went to my grandfather's house to ask if that was a good deal and to find out what he thought. I wondered if he had the money, so I asked him if he did, and he showed me this passbook he kept on the bookshelf behind the table, and it showed that he had a balance of $370,000 saved up. I remember thinking, "Wow, my grandfather is rich! That's a lot of money." After sharing the deal the ladies had offered to purchase their home and belongings, my grandfather told me to go and offer them $25,000, and see if they would accept.

They did not accept the $25,000 unfortunately, and instead sold the property for over $40,000. They had an estate sale, which also garnered more than $5,000. And they sold the car in their garage for $2,000. All in all, they made almost $50K. I told my grandfather.

Then life began, as it tends to do. The property was up for sale again less than four years later, now for $70,000. So, I went to see my grandfather and I asked him again. "What do you think we should offer?" He replied, "Offer them $40,000."

Again, the property was sold for more than that. While talking to my grandfather, I asked him how much he had saved up now. I thought it would have been way more than the $370,000 I had remembered seeing a few years prior. He pulled out his trusted passbook to show me, but to my surprise, his account balance had dropped to $250,000. It had not gone up at all. He was living off of his cash balance, and no real income was being generated with the capital, so it was just slowly dwindling down. The cost of living had increased, along with the cost of housing.

When my grandfather eventually passed away, I was asked if I could look over my grandmother's finances. I realized that she had a little less than $140,000 left at the time. And that property next door that we could have purchased twice was now worth well over $180,000. My grandparents never did invest their money or put their money to work for them, and their savings quickly eroded.

What I experienced was a valuable lesson on inflation. When capital is complacent and not invested somewhere, it will lose its purchasing power. I will always value this important lesson in my life. It really taught me the value of putting capital to work.

My grandparents Emidio and Carmella D'Orazio (1995) with me, Daniel and Nicholas

THE RULE OF SEVENTY-TWO

One of the most important rules we ever learned with investing was the rule of seventy-two. The rule of seventy-two is a basic formula that tells you how long (in years) it will take to double your money in value at a specified annual interest rate. This is important when you begin investing your money, which is my ultimate hope for you. In order to do this calculation, you simply need to divide the number seventy-two by the interest rate you are working with to find out approximately how many years it will take before your investment doubles in value. As an example, if you were to invest $10,000 at 6 percent interest, it would take 12 years for your money to double (simply divide 72 by 6). You can also use the rule of seventy-two to determine the interest rate needed to double your money within a specified amount of time. For example, to double your money in 10 years, you would require an annual interest rate of 7.2 percent (72 divided by 10 equals 7.2). The rule of seventy-two isn't an exact science, and is more of an approximation, but it is accurate enough for you to use it for your investments to calculate how long they will take before yielding a good return. Many people use the rule of seventy-two on a regular basis to assess and analyze their investment deals before committing to the terms.

LIVING WITHIN YOUR MEANS

North America differs from many other countries around the world because we have become attached and accustomed to the idea of credit – making large purchases for things that we otherwise wouldn't be able to purchase without credit. This is a dangerous game and gets many families into deep financial debt. Credit is important to have for emergencies and in situations where a credit card is required, but living on credit and spending on credit routinely is asking for trouble. We truly need to learn to live within our means. We often talk to our clients about this because it seems that many do not understand exactly what that means, especially if they have never done it.

Living within your means does not mean starving yourself, eating ramen, and having no social life. It simply means looking at your budget, paying all of your bills *first*, and then using what remains as your means of entertainment, rather than using a credit card. Credit cards make us complacent. We defer thinking about how we are going to pay for something when we use a credit card, because we don't have to. And credit card companies aren't in the business of having their customers pay off their cards; in fact, they hope that you won't. They make way more money when you don't pay off your cards and are late, or only pay the minimum each month. The industry thrives on struggle, and you have to know this every time you reach for that card. The credit card companies do not have your best interest at heart; it is not like free money, and it is going to be a challenge to pay off. Instead of instinctively reaching for your credit card, why not instead make your major purchasing decisions in advance and budget for them? Plan them out and set aside some of your savings each month to account for the purchase. That way, you can pay for things with money that you have saved and planned for. It is also important to ask yourself if you really *need* those big-ticket items or if you just *want* them.

There is a distinct difference here. Of course, if your refrigerator just craps out on you and dies, you may have no choice but to use credit or dip into your savings account. But if you are starting to think you want a newer, bigger stainless-steel fridge with an icemaker, but your current fridge is still fully operational and fine, then plan for a future purchase. Don't replace expensive items simply because you feel like it unless you really have your finances together and in order. If you plan on purchasing a big-ticket item, don't use your credit card or a department store card to do it. It will take years for you to pay off that item. But when you plan it out, save some money each month, and then go into the store in four months' time to make the purchase, you are in a much better position.

You may also feel much better inside when you know that you are in a position of power. You are not relying on the store to finance your purchase or your credit card to cover the cost; you have cold, hard cash in your hands, and you are ready to buy. Notice within you how different that feels than when you finance something on store credit – a totally different energy that makes you feel at ease and at peace with yourself. When we make large purchases on store credit or with credit cards, we feel a slight discomfort sometimes, because deep inside of us, we know that it isn't helping us or doing us any favours to buy something with money we don't have. Your intuition is a wonderful guide if you just listen to it.

Your budget will help you determine what living within your means really means. If you haven't created a family budget and don't know how much you have coming in and going out each month, how could you possibly know how much you have to live on? You won't. So, budgeting is an essential part of regaining control of your finances. Make sure that you have paid for your fixed expenses, your groceries, and your bills before you go spending money on things like clothes, dining out, and entertainment. Also make sure that you are setting at least 5 percent of your monthly income aside for savings or in case an emergency crops up in the future. If you simply pay your bills and spend what's left on fun and entertainment, you will be in a bad situation if anything unexpected pops up and surprises you. And we all know, it happens. Your car could give you mechanical problems, a major appliance could die, a family member could pass away, or your home may require extensive repair in some way. This is life, and these things happen. So as long as you have a plan in place, you will be fine.

Living within your means also brings more quality to the things you do. When you live unconsciously with money, unaware of how much things cost and how much you are spending, you don't truly appreciate what you have and what you spend money on. But when you know that you have a specific amount set aside each month for dining out with friends, you will make the most of those experiences and will come to appreciate them more, rather than taking them for granted. And you will feel way more confident about having paid your bills, having put some aside, and being able to go out for a nice meal.

GINA ON THE IMPORTANCE OF CREDIT

There are many factors that go into deciding whether you will get approved for a loan. One of the more important factors is credit. Lenders use this as a way of gauging the creditworthiness of a potential borrower, which provides an estimate of the chance of default and consequently, the risk of financial loss for the lender.

When viewing a client's credit report it gives you a sense of what has been happening in their life. We may see arrears on credit cards, loans, or mortgages, that could be an isolated incident stemming from a job loss, divorce, or sickness. These are easier to explain than a client who just consistently does not pay on time.

Over the years, we have worked with many clients, coaching them on how to improve their credit to prepare them for a future house purchase or using this to get them in a better financial situation overall, because having bad credit when applying for a loan will limit your capacity to borrow or provide a less than ideal rate, which will increase your overall monthly mortgage payments.

Here are a few tips and recommendations we have made to our clients over the years when it comes to managing credit.

- *Try not to run your balances up to the credit limit. Instead, keep your account balances below 75 percent of your available credit. This helps your credit score.*

- *You don't need ten credit cards! Pick two or three that you like, have and establish a limit of at least $5,000. I've seen people with a couple of credit cards and a limit of only $1,000. Sure, your credit score number might be good in that scenario, but it is not enough for a lender to make a judgment on your credit worthiness.*

- *Make your payments on time! Even just the minimum payment. I've seen credit cards with a balance of $1,000 and minimum payments of $10 not being made—and it ruins your credit, believe it or not!*

- *Don't apply for too much credit — too many inquiries in a short period of time and lenders will think you are a credit seeker and will penalize you for it.*

- *Use credit, even if it is for small gas purchases. People think that if they don't use credit that they will have a great credit score, which is not true.*

- *If you are thinking of buying a house in the next couple of years, it's a great idea to regularly check your credit through Equifax or Transunion.*

If you're a parent, teach your kids the importance of credit and help get them started when they are old enough to obtain credit. The quicker you can establish credit and build a robust bureau which includes loans, credit cards, and lines of credit, and are making payments on time, the quicker you will increase your chances of getting approved for future loans.

I've seen many clients that we have worked with personally that have taken this advice and improved their credit scores substantially. It really is a great feeling when you assist people in changing their financial picture, and they transform their lives from being in a place where they don't have enough money to creating wealth and disposable income that can be put into savings. It's about keeping life simple!

WHEN YOUR CREDIT SCORE IS POOR

As we discussed, credit should never be used in place of cash unless absolutely necessary. Credit is a wonderful safety net to use in case of an emergency or for occasional convenience situations where a credit card is required. But if you have gone on a wild spending spree with your cards for the last few years and now you are struggling to make the minimum payments each month, you are going to have to commit to stopping your spending.

First, decide which card to pay off first. Which card are you paying the highest interest on? Often, these are department store cards. Commit to paying those down faster by paying more than the minimum. If you can cut the card up before you pay it off, do it. If not, pay off the card and then cut the card up. Second, decide which credit card you would like to keep for emergencies and occasional use. Usually, the lowest-interest card is the wisest choice. Third, determine how much you want to have available on the card. If your limit is $20,000 and you are afraid you might spend, reduce the limit by cutting it in half. Finally, in order to get your credit back on track, you are going to have to show consistent progress with making payments on your cards. And remember that even the cards that you pay off will still show on your file as a liability if you do not get rid of them. For this reason, it is essential to minimize the number of credit cards you have. Only keep one or two at most. The rest you should pay off and get rid of. Make sure that you actually close your account once the card has been paid off. If you simply pay off a card and think that your account is closed, you are kidding yourself.

The amount of credit on the card is considered a liability until you actually close the account and no longer have that credit available to you. Some credit card companies make closing your account difficult because they don't want you to pay off your cards and close your account. That's not how they make money. But it's how you will regain good credit and get control of your finances. It takes time to rebuild poor credit, but with a proper plan in place, you can do it over a period of time, with regular payments and communication with your creditors. Ignoring them when you don't have their money doesn't make them go away or not report you, but if you just pick up the phone and negotiate with them, they are often more than willing to work with you if you have a bad month.

Remember, the objective of creating positive cash flow is increasing the amount of cash you have available to you. Whether you do this by consolidating your debts, reducing your spending, or increasing your revenue streams, it is an essential component to building wealth and regaining control of your finances. Having liquid cash available to you is a huge asset and will help you in all areas of your life, making your life less stressful and far more manageable.

JOE'S RULE OF SEVENTY-TWO STORY

When I look back at a personal lesson about investing in cash flow, I remember that growing up in our family, debt was a bad thing to have. Therefore, you had to get out of debt as fast as possible by saving your money to pay down your debt and be very frugal with your spending until that debt was paid. Once we became debt-free, then a percentage of the income we earned could go toward investments instead of debt. And that's how wealth was built.

I had a client who came to me (let's call him John). He was self-employed and didn't have the taxable income that the bank required to lend money to him. He wanted to purchase a commercial property, and needed funding for the purchase. I arranged a mortgage for $140,000 at a rate of 12 percent, with fees representing 3 percent of the loan. He thought the rate was too high, and that he would be paying too much in fees, so he asked me if I knew anyone else. I went to a realtor friend, who proposed we fund it fifty-fifty, which meant I would need to come up with $70,000. I only had $32,000 saved up in my savings account at the time, so I looked at my line of credit, which was $50,000. The rate that I was paying was 6 percent. So, bingo, I was able to do it. I called up my client and funded his mortgage at 10 percent, with a 1 percent fee. The realtor and I together funded the mortgage on time, for a better rate, and the client was happy.

That was the first mortgage I ever funded independently. I was able to borrow a portion of the money from the bank and then use the payments that the client made to me directly to pay down my borrowed money. When time passed, I noticed that my line of credit was paid off. So I was reset again, but my investment was still worth $70,000.

That was my first leverage loan, and with the rule of seventy-two on my side, I paid off the borrowed money in half the time. But what about the client? What happened to him? That was a win-win situation. He successfully sold the property seven years later for over $700,000.

He showed me up on that investment. The rule of seventy-two actually proved to be more successful and profitable owning the property than on the debt itself. Mine was close to a double, and the client was close to a triple. To this day, he is still one of my good friends.

GINA'S REFLECTIONS ON CASH FLOW

When I worked as an employee, I relied on a steady paycheque and a great pension. This was always my go-to plan. Having witnessed my parents loyally work their whole lives for a company until they reached retirement, I thought I would follow the same path. My parents were both able to retire in their late fifties with a good pension, so I always valued that as a pretty good approach. But life changes and doesn't always create the path you think it will, and becoming self-employed with my husband was a great move for us. It was important for us to start putting together a plan for an income stream when we did retire. This planning has been an ongoing discussion between Joe and I which we started in our late thirties, early forties. We'd have regular discussions about how much money we would need during our retirement. We'd try to determine what our expenses would be and how we would accomplish our financial goals to feel secure and comfortable when we were ready to retire. This thinking and planning has been a cornerstone of our relationship and something we've always aligned on.

One of the ways Joe and I sought cash flow was to invest in real estate. My dream has always been to have one apartment building in our portfolio generating a healthy stream of monthly revenue. I saw this as a smart way of creating passive and sustainable cash flow that we could rely on later on in life. That dream became a reality for us in 2008. We found a great small apartment building in a good location with long-term tenants. The property didn't immediately provide us with positive cash flow, as we had a lot to learn and made some mistakes along the way. We were pushed out of our comfort zones multiple times and felt scared and worried, but we embraced the challenge and continued to grow. Over time, as we learned the ropes and figured things out, it became a good source of revenue and proved to be a sound financial decision and a good investment in our future.

I have seen, over the years, clients who have the capacity and income to grow and be very successful but who fall down because they get too accustomed to the status quo and are too worried to jump into the unknown or push themselves to go the extra mile when they're already tired. To clarify, stepping outside your comfort zone doesn't mean that you need to dive headfirst into something you have no idea about to see if you sink or swim. Stepping out of your comfort zone is about pushing yourself to the next rung in the ladder. I apply this concept to my exercise regimen. I push myself to increase my strength when handling weights or to be able to run faster even when I'm feeling tired. It helps me to become stronger and faster over time, instead of just accepting where I'm at, staying there, and never pushing myself – which wouldn't increase strength or stamina. The same is true in life and finance. You have to be adaptable and flexible, and that will help you to build your confidence once you become good at it.

We are constantly taking on new challenges – sometimes by choice and sometimes because an investment is not going well, and we have no choice but to step in and resolve the problem. You can never be complacent and comfortable – these are killers of progress. It's easy to spend our time looking in the past at all the things we've accomplished and say, "I'm done! I made it!" But we don't stay in that mode for long. We appreciate what we have built but success does not mean it'll still be there tomorrow.

For the most part, Joe and I have always aligned on cash flow matters. I can recall a time early in our marriage that he spent a considerable amount of money on a car repair that he did not tell me about. I was on maternity leave at the time, and my income was reduced, so we had to be more careful. The repair could have waited until I was back at work, since our cash flow was reduced. I was upset with him because we had not discussed it beforehand, and he just went ahead and paid for it without thinking about how it affected our budget and cash flow. We talked about it afterward and both agreed to always communicate in advance when something comes up, so there's no surprises and we can plan for things together.

You need to communicate with your partner. Agree and commit to only spend a certain amount each week or month on personal purchases. Have a shared goal that works for both people in the relationship. Basic needs always come first, of course – you have to prioritize needs before you and your partner negotiate the wants. There is no one right way to manage money as a couple, so the best thing to do is talk through options and pick the one that works best for your situation. You are never going to agree on absolutely everything when it comes to money and cash flow, but talking about it is important. Consistent financial problems can lead to resentment, secrecy, and anger down the road, and wreak havoc on a relationship.

Never take your cash flow for granted. Always think ahead, prepare, and plan. This is how you will create financial security for your family. You have to keep working on it day after day, altering course when needed, never becoming complacent or thinking you can skip the budget this month. That leads to problems. One of our clients shared a saying with us that we still use today, and that is, "the process of refinement never ends" – because every day is a day to improve on yesterday, to learn and grow into a better person. Your financial health will improve with daily focus and attention to detail.

ATTITUDE

One of the most important things you can do for yourself is become aware of how your attitude affects each situation and outcome in your life. Attitude plays a huge role in your overall success as a person and can truly make or break you. We have met people in our lives who were very successful financially, but who struggled immensely in other areas of their lives due to their attitude. Just having money but being unable to attract loving relationships, give of yourself, or experience gratitude is not the hallmark of a successful individual. What makes a successful person is someone who embraces a healthy attitude toward life and success, and someone who has a bit of humility about themselves. Things aren't always going to work out the way you think they will, and it's what you do in those moments that matters. If you handle it well, you will grow, evolve, and become a better person. But if you crumble, criticize, or become negative and jaded, you will only hurt yourself by allowing that type of attitude to perpetuate itself within you, eating away at your spirit and taking away from your success as a person.

Of course, you will have those days when your attitude just plain sucks, and you know it sucks, but you can't seem to snap out of it. But each time we bring awareness to our attitude, we create the opportunity to change it, so the amount of time you spend on negativity and self-pity will decrease each time you consciously think about how your attitude is helping or hurting you. When you aren't sure, simply ask yourself the question, *"Is my attitude helping or hurting me in this moment?"* If the latter, do something to shift into a more positive mindset – even if it means not thinking about the situation at hand.

HEALTHY INNER DIALOGUE

Each of us has a voice within that walks around with us all day, thinking, feeling, and expressing opinions. This voice, unfortunately, doesn't always have our best interests at heart. It is sometimes a negative voice that operates from fear rather than love. It is very important that we acknowledge when our inner dialogue needs to change, because if those messages we hear each day are negative, then we are going to walk around feeling negative. The universe works in such a way that we attract what we think about most. So if our predominant thoughts are negative in nature, then the experiences and situations we find ourselves in will often be negative, and we will wonder why we are so unlucky. Often, negative people don't see the connection between so-called luck and their own attitude. Luck has nothing to do with it. The people who experience success and who have positive experiences work hard to keep their attitude positive and focus on supporting themselves with a healthy inner dialogue.

Most of our inner dialogue stems from messages we received about ourselves as children. If we felt left out, picked on, or unimportant, those messages often stayed with us into adulthood. Those messages then become beliefs, which is dangerous. If we allow old feelings from childhood to manifest into adult beliefs, they can cause a lot of damage in our lives and prevent us from our own success. It is important that we release those thoughts and feelings so that we can move forward positively. Observe your inner dialogue, frequently making notes about how your inner voice is either helping or hurting you. Each time you notice a negative dialogue, ask yourself if this dialogue has come up before. More than likely, it is an old, familiar tape that has been playing for years. Our inner voice often operates on autopilot and simply plays, on a loop, all of the negative and unhealthy things that we have always allowed it to tell us – for example, if you are about to embark on something new and you notice the voice telling you to quit because you will probably fail anyway, or telling you that you can't do what you are about to do.

Observe the voice without judgment. Simply notice the dialogue and then replace the unhealthy message with a healthier one, such as, "Growth happens when I step outside of my comfort zone," or "This is going to be an exciting new experience." It is important to replace the unhealthy dialogue with positive thoughts because, over time, the volume of the negative inner voice will become less and less and the volume of the positive thoughts will become greater, creating a new healthy inner dialogue.

Financial well-being is one of those areas that lends itself well to self-criticism and negative inner dialogue. If you have failed in the past at managing your finances, your credit, or paying your bills, it is possible that you already have a negative inner dialogue about your financial health. Before you can work to change this dialogue, it is important that you identify it.

IDENTIFYING YOUR FINANCIAL INNER DIALOGUE

Grab a notebook and a pen and write down the following headings: income, bills, money management, potential for wealth, and success. Underneath each heading, write down your thoughts and feelings about that topic as they occur to you. Think about how each topic relates to you and your life. If you have negative inner dialogue, you will quickly notice that your notes are negative, fearful, unconfident, and stressful. It is important that you recognize that this unhealthy and negative inner dialogue stems from past experiences and has no place or business in the present moment. You are living right now. What has happened is gone, even if you are still paying the price for past mistakes. You simply have to move forward from this point on. Changing your inner dialogue is paramount. If you have written down unhealthy notes under each financial topic, replace them with something more positive. If you feel negative about doing it, make it something that you can believe in, such as, "I am working towards a life where cash flow is easy and plentiful." Recite these positive mantras each day for a few minutes in the morning before you begin your day.

POSITIVITY

We are human, and because of that, we don't always feel wonderful and inspired. We will inevitably have good days and bad days, but when we can focus on becoming a more positive and optimistic person, the bad days become less prevalent in our lives. Our challenges become opportunities for growth instead of just plain bad luck. Those who have a positive outlook on things experience less stress and illness in their lives than those who are negative. Stress and negativity create disease in our lives, and can contribute to a number of health ailments. But positivity isn't only good for your body, mind, and spirit – it is also good for your wallet.

Positive people tend to get back up on the horse and try again when faced with adversity. That willingness to walk it off is what propels them to succeed. If you get too hung up on what happened in the past and focused on why things didn't work out and who is to blame, you are missing the opportunity to grow and become better. The true lessons in life come from our failures. If we were successful at everything we set out to do, victory wouldn't be all that worthwhile. It wouldn't be as sweet. But when we take risks, try, fail a few times, and get back up again, it feels wonderful when we reach the summit.

Positive thinking helps us to see our life experience in a different way. Instead of getting down on ourselves when we make a mistake or experience a setback, we learn from the situation and continue to move forward without allowing the experience to damage us. Positivity is daily work. It isn't something that you just get once and keep forever. It is hard work for even the most seasoned optimist. Because let's face it, life is unpredictable, and we can't always control what happens. So things will inevitably happen that we aren't prepared for, don't want, and can't control. That is the nature of being a human being on this planet. But the way that we manage those challenges is truly what matters.

Positivity can not only help our relationships, happiness, and quality of life, but our financial life, too. The way we think and relate to money is a big factor in our ability to manage money, make money, and accumulate wealth. Often, the people who struggle the most live in constant fear of losing what they have, and they constantly feel that there isn't enough and that there will never be enough. When you are focused on what you don't have instead of what you have, you simply invite more of that negative, lacking energy into your life. The universe delivers what you think about most. So, if your predominant thoughts are centered on not having enough money and being in financial trouble, then you will continue to experience that. But as soon as you shift your thoughts and begin to make small positive changes, you will notice that climbing out of that is much easier. It doesn't matter how much money you make or don't make, you are capable of changing your situation.

How to think positively about your finances:

- **Set some realistic goals.**
  Talk to your spouse or partner and sit down together to discuss what you have coming in and calculate what you have going out. Consider consolidating your bills, cutting out extra expenses, or lowering your

expenses wherever possible. Write down your goals on paper and agree to work toward them with your partner.

- **If you slip, get back up.**
  If you happen to have a month where you slipped a little or had to pay for unexpected expenses, don't let that drag you down; simply adjust your budget and move forward. Don't come down hard on yourself or your partner; instead, resolve to stick to your financial plan and stay on target. You will feel much better for doing so. Resist the urge to point the finger and blame your partner, and instead, make sure you are on the same page.

- **Create positive affirmations.**
  You have goals that you are working toward to get your finances on track and in good shape, so now you must train your mind to think positively about these goals. Create some affirmations about your finances and memorize them. Any time you notice yourself going down the wrong thought path with money matters, quickly replace the negative thought with one of your positive affirmations. At first, it may feel forced and superficial, but with regular practice, your positive affirmations will far outweigh your negative thoughts, and you will begin to manifest positive results.

- **Focus on the present.**
  Stay in the present moment and resist the urge to feel bad or depressed about spending that has already occurred. The bills are what they are, and there is no changing that. You must work to move forward. Think about paying them off and see that happening. Don't blame anyone for spending unnecessarily if it has already happened; instead, put a plan in place for the future for big purchases. Agree to save either partially or fully before putting things on credit. Staying present with your thoughts will help you to continue to be positive and stay focused on your goals, rather than thinking about the mistakes or events that lead you to be where you are. You cannot change the past, but you can absolutely change the future, beginning right now with the very thoughts you have in your head.

- **Create small rewards.**
  If you stay on budget, reward yourself at the end of each week with a

romantic dinner for you and your partner, either made at home or out at a restaurant if budget permits. Acknowledge the positive changes in your financial behaviour and reward yourself in a controlled way by predetermining the rewards and accounting for them in your budget. By tying the reward to your ability to stay on budget, you are demonstrating that you are in control of your finances, which will perpetuate feelings of success and positivity. Buying things that we don't budget for often makes us feel guilty or frivolous, which doesn't help us to get better. But when we plan and budget for the things we need, the whole energy of the transaction changes. Rewards can be monthly expenditures, occasional dinners, bigger-ticket items, or weekly date nights. Figure out what works best for your family and budget.

HOW TO LOSE MONEY WITH STYLE BY JOE

"Joe, you need to learn to lose money with style." This was told to me by a friend, Bruno after losing close to 80 percent of my savings. Yes, you read that right: 80 percent of my life's savings. It was catastrophic.

Bruno called me one day after I successfully concluded a lawsuit I had been embroiled in. I had won the case, but it didn't feel great considering what I had just spent on legal fees and the not-so-small fact that I was still 80 percent down on my savings doing what turned out to be a terrible business deal. He asked me what I was doing over the weekend. He asked, "Why don't you go to New York City? Wake up in the morning with your wife and have breakfast at Tiffany's?" I was thoroughly confused about what he was saying. Was he asking me to go to New York, I wondered. Maybe he and his wife were going. I didn't know what the intent behind his words were at that moment. But he continued on: "Mr. Trombetta, you have already lost all of that money. So what's another $10,000 for you?" Suddenly, I got what he was saying. "Joe, you need to learn to lose money with style," he said.

The punchline is, in order for you to make money, you must master the art of losing money with style. I've never forgotten those words he shared with me that day, and I thanked him for taking the time to share that phrase, because it's had a huge impact on my life and my attitude toward losing money.

If you want to be in the money business, you gotta learn to go with the flow. Sometimes you lose, sometimes you win – and you should never put yourself in a situation where you aren't prepared to handle either of those outcomes.

Don't put all your eggs in one basket. Share your risk with your partners, share the rewards, and share those experiences.

Remember, even in the money business, it's not all about the money.

Everyone loses money. We live in a society where money is earned, spent, lost, exchanged, and saved. And losing money is just part of the game — especially if you become involved in the stock market. Successful traders know that failure is just par for the course and all part of the job. You would be hard pressed to find a trader who has never lost money or lost an account. They simply don't exist. All traders have lost money. But it's not the fact that they lose money that matters, it's how quickly they recover. That is really what differentiates the amateur and the professional. The amateur licks their wounds and shies away from future deals, remembering the loss. They let the loss define them, and the energy of that loss seeps out of their pores. The professional takes it as a learning opportunity and continues to invest fearlessly, knowing that there may be another loss in the future, but that there will also likely be wins. They move forward with confidence, and don't let the loss define them.

Whether you lost money on a bad investment, lent it to a friend, or simply spent your life savings, the fact remains: that money is gone. It doesn't mean that you won't earn it back, or that you will never be successful again — it just means that you must look forward. And when you do look forward, it is possible that something bigger and better is right around the corner for you. Don't live in the darkness of your financial failures, because it will be impossible to find the light if you do that. Instead, take it as a learning opportunity, no matter the circumstance, and know that there will be good days and bad days, but that you will be able to handle whatever comes your way. Learn to control the things that make you better (like your spending, your saving habits, and creating cash flow) and learn to accept the things that you cannot control. There will be financial surprises. Life is full of them. Once you accept that, you will be in a much better position to succeed. Don't take a loss as a devastating defeat.

Money is simply energy, constantly flowing and constantly moving. Sometimes you have a lot, other times it is tied up, and sometimes you want more. Whatever the case, know that money is energy, and your attitude toward that energy is what defines how successful you are. If you allow the energy of money to create anxiety and depression within you every time something unexpected happens, you will not be a very good player in this game of life. However, if you see money for what it is and allow your attitude to reflect that, you will come out on top.

ENVISION SUCCESS

A huge part of being successful is believing that you will be. If you simply want to be successful but, inside you, hold a limiting belief that you will never achieve success, then success will never come to you, because your beliefs will not allow it. You have to feel with every fibre of your being that you are worthy and deserving of success and know that it is there for the taking. If you do not believe that you will ever be successful or believe that you are unworthy in any way, you, my friend, have a hard road ahead of you. Simply wanting is not enough, you have to believe and know that with your thoughts, you pave the road to your future success. Your thoughts will attract your reality, not your wants. There are plenty of people in the world who want to make a six-figure salary, but they never actually get there because inside, they don't believe they are worth it and they don't do the work required to change their thoughts. Thinking negatively about yourself results in a negative experience. You have to envision the life you want for yourself and see it happening. The more specific and clear your thoughts are about envisioning what you want, the more realistic the chances of you attaining your goals.

It is important to set your goals in stages so that you can feel good about yourself when you attain success. If you are making $40K per year and set a goal for yourself to have $100K saved by the end of the year, you are going to be pretty disappointed when it doesn't happen. But it isn't a realistic goal. Envision realistic goals as well as larger ones. Let the small steps be the ones that lead you to your overall life goal. For example, if your dream is to own a five-bedroom home by the lake, then work to envision small steps. Start by saving 10 percent of your monthly salary and putting it aside, sticking to your budget each month, researching property values in the area that you want to live, taking a drive in the neighbourhood, looking at homes, and thinking about which ones appeal to you. While dreaming about that home beside the lake and allowing yourself to go and look at them, you are also doing the very real work of saving your money and sticking to your budget. Eventually, you will have money for a down payment, will be in a good credit situation, and will be in a position to get pre-approved for a mortgage.

Joe receiving CIPBA Award for Excellence in Business Leadership (2021), left to right Gina, Cesidio and Maria Trombetta, and Joe

How to envision your success:

- Get as close to what you want as you can without getting it.
- Learn and do research about your goals by reading.
- Meditate and visualize yourself accomplishing your goals.

- Use positive affirmations to recite to yourself each day.
- Do the work required to get to where you want to be.
- Set smaller, realistic baby goals that work toward your overall objective.
- Acknowledge the success you've had along the way.
- Tell people what your dreams and goals are – make it real.
- Talk to people who are experiencing or living your goals and learn from them.
- Allow your goals to be flexible when they need to change.
- Do one thing each day that supports your dreams and goals in some way.

THE ART OF INFLUENCE

There is something that can be even more powerful than money, and that thing is called influence. With influence we can learn, get help from others, advance faster, and ultimately get to where we want to be. By leveraging the art of influence, we learn how to get to people who can help us. Just a quick scan of your LinkedIn contacts will show you that you are probably a lot more influential than you thought. But when was the last time you searched through your contacts and asked yourself what they have or do that could be of value to you? This doesn't mean taking without giving; this is about learning how to leverage your contacts in an intelligent way so that you can gain from their knowledge, expertise, or influence. Ask yourself, also, what you can do for your contacts. Influence is a two-way street. You cannot be willing to take from people but give nothing back in return; you must also offer your time, knowledge, expertise, and help others. This is how to build influence.

One of the longest-held secrets of the social elite when it comes to being influential and getting what you want is a simple but important point: **you must ask for what you want**. Some people sit around wondering how others have access to successful people, get them to endorse their projects or work, or have them in their sphere of influence. Successful people get asked for help, and eventually those people who asked for help become both influential and successful themselves. You, too, can be influential by beginning to ask for what you want. Look at your contacts and the people in your life and who they are connected to. Is there a link between where you are trying to go and who these people are? If so, ask them if they can spare a few minutes to have a conversation with you. There is no harm in asking. Ask them if there is anything you can do for them, and offer your own time and expertise in return.

left to right, Joe, Joe Mancinelli, PM Justin Trudeau (2013)

Knowing the right person is often the hardest part. How do you get to the person who has what you want? This is where you have to do your legwork. Talk to people and tell them what you are trying to accomplish, whatever it is. Ask them if they have any recommendations for someone you can talk to. And when you find that person, try to get together with them in person, rather than emailing them. Invite them for a coffee or a breakfast meeting, or if they cannot do that, ask them if they have a few minutes to meet via video chat. Show them that you appreciate them taking the time and offer to help them out because you don't want to build a reputation for being a taker. Before you begin making asks of people, why not first offer yourself? Look for volunteer work, offer to help start-up companies with your unique expertise, help a charity, promote your friends' books and businesses on your social media platforms, or acknowledge the success of your friends and network publicly. And most importantly, take the time to meet with people face to face and listen to them. Hear them out and understand what is going on in their lives without thinking about what you want from them.

Being an honest and caring person is paramount to building influence. You have to care about others, be willing to help, and be grateful. You also have to know where to spend your time and not give too much of your time to people who don't reciprocate. Sometimes, people ask too much of others, and they just bounce from contact to contact asking for what they want until someone gives it to them. But this eventually exhausts their contact list, and they end up alone. It is always easy to spot someone who never gives back. They may get away with it once or twice, but it eventually catches up with them and stops working. It also creates the kind of negative karma and energy that stops you from getting what you want.

You can always choose to help people, and there is almost always something that you can do to give back when others help you, even if that just means acknowledging their help by sending them a gift or taking them out to dinner. People like to feel acknowledged and appreciated, especially when they help others achieve success. Think about the ways in which you are in a position to help others. If you are financially well, you can offer your investment in ideas and companies. If you are a successful executive, you can offer your time. If you have experience working in a specific industry, you can offer your expertise. And all of us are capable of lending a hand and an ear, which is often the most helpful of all. Never put others on a pedestal and think that because they have achieved more, have more, or do more, that they are above you. We are all human beings on different paths.

Some of us are at different stages of our lives and have experienced some success along the way, but it doesn't mean that you aren't worthy or aren't going to get there yourself. See yourself as being on that trajectory and leverage the art of influence to help you get there. Work on building your network and talking to people. Get comfortable with asking – it's the only way to get to a yes. You can't expect to get what you want without asking, or by doing everything alone. We all need help sometimes.

<u>Remember these tips for building influence:</u>

- If you don't ask, you won't get answers.
- Don't be afraid to reach out to people.
- Help others and be a good listener.
- Know the value of your contacts and network.
- Speak up if there is something you need.
- Know where and how to spend your time.

- Reciprocate and work with others who do the same.
- Don't shy away from conflict. See it as a growth opportunity.
- Think positively about accessing the people who can help you.

TURNING A NEGATIVE INTO A POSITIVE: JOE'S STORY

I remember an incident well over fifteen years ago that I took extremely personally. I had lent money to a client and due to circumstances in his life, he was unfortunately unable to pay me back. Feeling burned, I quickly hired a lawyer to begin the process of trying to get this money back. I wasn't willing to listen or work with him any longer, as I perceived him as just continuing to lie and cheat and avoid his responsibility.

After a long and stressful court case, I finally won and felt some sense of satisfaction in the matter. But this quickly faded, because I didn't actually get my money back. My lawyer took it. I spent so much time going after this guy to seek justice that I spent the money he owed me on legal fees, so in the end, nobody truly won.

A short time later, I went to a friend of mine, Tom, for some advice. I told him that I had a new situation with a guy who wasn't paying me what he owed for a home I had mortgaged for him privately, and that I was unfortunately going to have to pursue legal action against him. I told him that I was worried that I was going to lose money again paying exorbitant legal fees. He looked at me and paused, and said, "Joe, why don't you just pay for the moving truck?"

Joe and Tom Hoan (2014)

I was shocked. "What? Can I do that?" That thought hadn't even remotely entered my mind. At that moment, I learned about not taking things so personally – especially when someone can't pay you what they owe you, because you never really know what's going on in someone's life behind closed doors. It was a breakthrough moment for me.

From there, I chose to work one-on-one with the client who couldn't pay me, and I did so with a little bit of empathy for the situation. I went to see him and told him that I was willing to work with him. I told him that it was obvious he could no longer afford to stay in his home, but that I wanted him to succeed and was willing to help. I offered to help him right-size his home so he could get into something he could afford, given his financial trouble. This client turned around and looked at me with a huge amount of gratitude in his eyes and said, "Thank you for saving my dignity. Thank you for allowing me to move on my own terms."

I could not believe the successful outcome in this previously bad situation. We relocated the client to his new home that he could now afford and paid for his moving expenses. This proved to be way cheaper than paying for a lawyer, and made me feel better about things.

This situation really gave me pause and made me change my attitude toward people in handling arrears and the sticky circumstances that occur when people run into financial trouble. Customers don't plan on missing their mortgage payments. They don't want or expect to, and if it happens, it's likely an incredibly stressful situation in their lives. I could now see this more clearly. Through acting with empathy and compassion and understanding the client's situation, but also being honest about where I was at, we were able to find a solution together.

It's especially important to keep your attitude about money and success in check when running a small business or living the entrepreneurship life. It can be very difficult facing a never-ending array of challenging situations. Problems occur often, decisions have to be made that aren't easy to make, and things can feel stressful at times. It is very similar to going to an amusement park and riding on a rollercoaster ride. There are plenty of ups and downs – it can feel scary, but also thrilling and joyful. We all encounter hard times, heartache, success, and failure. There are times that we are working with clients where we are not 100 percent sure if we will be able to get a deal approved for them, or get them the rates they expect. There is an inner dialogue that sometimes has to be fought that says, *"chances are we're going to work with this person, do all of this legwork for them, and they will not end up using our services in the end."* This is negative thinking that is self-destructive and defeatist. This may be due to previous experiences with clients that used our time and knowledge and then decided to go elsewhere, leaving us feeling burned. In these moments, it's important that we remind ourselves that it's crucial to keep a positive attitude and to take a leap of faith. People are worth believing in, and as long as we are self-motivated and continue to be encouraging, that is a success, no matter the outcome.

GINA ON THE IMPORTANCE OF ATTITUDE

A few years ago, I was at a social function and a young lady came up to me and said, "You may not remember me, but you did my mortgage. My husband and I were so nervous, but you kept reassuring us and made us feel so much better by telling us that things would all work out. Your positive attitude made a big difference." This was such a great compliment because it wasn't about the mortgage, the work, or the outcome, it was about how I made them feel during that important period of time – a point in time when they were making one of the biggest decisions of their lives.

I am quite a positive person in general, but I'm also a human being, so it's not always like that. I have moments where I feel overwhelmed, frustrated, angry, or even disappointed. The way I deal with this is by going for a walk, unwinding, and engaging in activities that relax both my mind and body. Joe and I try to take small and frequent trips away, because it helps us to unplug from the daily stress while also stepping back to think about the big picture and how it aligns with our business. It reconnects our desires and goals as entrepreneurs and reaffirms the mission of our company.

I believe that we all have an intrinsic attitude towards money and the majority of our foundational beliefs come from our parents and their attitude toward money. As children we look at our parents and how they deal with their financial matters, and we pick up cues. Even though as children, we are too young to understand all of the intricacies involved with managing financial matters, the general sense of how organized or stressful money is in the family leaves a lasting impression.

My parents grew up in Italy during the Second World War. They were farmers and relied on the food they grew and some livestock. During the war, they had very little food, and during WWII, had to live in the mountains to escape for a short period of time. There was no extra money available to buy shoes or clothing.

They worked hard when they came to Canada to get ahead. My parents were successful because they knew how to save and were able to make some smart real estate investments. These stories were told to us frequently and these early experiences formed a blueprint of my financial thinking.

In turn, we try to pass this thinking onto our sons. We have regular conversations with them about their spending and saving habits, and remind them that money doesn't grow on trees, so that they are mindful. Our kids are all independent adults who handle their own finances now, and for the most part. they have picked up some positive habits and attitudes from us. They may not always make the same choices that we make, but they do turn to us for guidance and recall some of the lessons we taught them. But they know that their decisions are ultimately their own.

I have come to realize over time that most successful people are passionate about what they do, and are rarely influenced by negativity. They are always learning, growing, and changing. And they seem to have the ability to overcome negative people and events with ease. Rather than dwelling on mistakes or things that happened in the past, they learn from them, adjust course, and move forward. Joe and I also try to embody this outlook on life. We have of course experienced negative events, tragedy, and hardship, but we try not to live in that energy, and instead learn something from it, and move forward in the best way we can.

Attitude truly is everything. Every day, we get to choose how we think and feel about things. A positive attitude is inspiring to others and will be contagious to all around you. It will also lead you to the most success you've ever had. Your attitude dictates the outcome of things and how well you recover from hardship and adversity. You can't avoid challenges in life, but you can certainly choose to handle it better by controlling your thoughts. Be the change that you want to see in your own life by changing the way you think about things. Magical things will happen and unfold for you when you do this. In fact, it is simply astonishing how quickly success comes to those who are willing to do the inner work required to change. Your attitude is one thing that you can control, so why not turn negative experiences into positive ones by changing your attitude? You have nothing to lose and everything to gain.

RELATIONSHIPS

The relationships we have with others plays a strong role in our financial well-being. We have a number of relationships that either directly or indirectly affect or influence our financial lives. Some may be obvious, while others are ones you may not have even considered. We all have at least a few people in our lives who directly impact the livelihood of our financial life. For most, this includes a boss or a business partner, a spouse, a parent, or sometimes even an investor. These are the obvious ones, and are rooted in the source of our income or the person we jointly manage our finances with. These people are involved in our financial livelihood, and they know the ins and outs of our finances and the hardships we face. These are important relationships to consider, and we will come back to them later in this chapter. But there are other financial relationships that are equally important.

Take, for example, the role of the personal banker. Many people are terrified to go into the bank and actually speak to a living, breathing person. Banks can be intimidating – especially when applying for a loan or line of credit that we aren't sure if we even qualify for. But when you establish a healthy relationship with a personal banker, you open yourself up to a relationship that can be very beneficial to you. They will come to know you and understand your family's unique dynamics, understand what you need and how much flexibility you have, and be able to advise you on the best course of action. If you don't feel comfortable having that sort of a relationship with a personal banker – or you worry that the turnover of staff in the bank branch is too high – find yourself a financial advisor, someone with whom you can sit down and plan for the future. We also like to refer to this person as your financial engineer, because they are responsible for crafting your investment strategy and helping you understand financial concepts that are crucial to building wealth. You need to be able to be candid and open with your financial advisor. You cannot worry about how things look, or feel that you have to hide anything from your advisor. Your advisor is the one who will be there to pull you out of financial hardship and help you get on your feet so that you can put money away, invest, and save for retirement. They won't be able to do this without knowing the complete picture of your finances.

Building a strong relationship with a financial advisor is probably one of the smartest financial moves you will make, aside from taking personal responsibility for your finances. Advisors help us think about things that we often forget, like how to write off more expenses at tax time, or how much to put into an RRSP, or even how much we should be able to save from our paycheque each month. Your advisor can work out a family budget with you and help you figure out how to pay off your credit cards and start a savings account with a decent interest rate. Then, once you have enough money to play with and want to begin investing, your advisor will help you create a diversified portfolio.

When we first begin to take control of our financial lives, it is important that we work with people who we can trust, look up to, and take advice from. When I was early in my career, there were many that I looked to for knowledge, advice, and input about the way I was running my business. I wanted to make sure that I was making the right decisions to bring my business to profitability faster. I knew that if I looked to the people who came before me and to business leaders who were successful entrepreneurs, I could take my cues from them. Never be afraid to find a mentor or a leader to learn from. If you can't find that person within your community, you can always look to the bookstore or search the Internet.

Think about what you are trying to do and seek out specific information to do that thing. If you are running a franchise business, find the experts in that field. If you are investing and playing the stock market, find notable entrepreneurs who do this well and learn from them. Even if you are just trying to figure out how to run your family's finances, there are still experts out there who specialize only in this area. It doesn't just have to be one mentor, either; you can have several for different areas of your financial life. Perhaps you meet with them in person as we do with our clients, or maybe they are entrepreneurs who you look up to in the community, or you read their blog. They can even be public figures who have made millions at what they do. To have a relationship with someone you can look up to financially doesn't always mean that you have to know them intimately. You can have an online relationship with someone by following their blog or Twitter feed and commenting every once in a while. Or you can feel like you are having a relationship with someone by reading their book. You don't have to figure everything out on your own.

There are people who have been where you are right now who can help you get to where you want to go. Think about what your goals are and who might be able to help you.

HOW TO NURTURE INFLUENTIAL FRIENDSHIPS

We talked a little bit about influence in the last section of the book when we discussed attitude, but now, let's talk about how to nurture those friendships so that you can have strong allies on your side that you can learn from. Everyone needs at least a few influential people in their lives to help them look at things with a unique perspective. These people might be friends or family members with successful businesses, executives you look up to, public figures, or very well connected people in the community. Most of us know at least one or two influential people, and often, a quick scan of our Facebook or LinkedIn account could identify who those people are, if you don't already know immediately.

Influential people can help you in a number of ways – by providing you with introductions to powerful people, giving you feedback or advice on business ideas or investment decisions, or simply being an advocate for the work you do. But just make sure that you don't go into these relationships expecting to take and not give. There is a right way and a wrong way to approach influential people. If they are already in your circle of friends but you have never asked much of them, that is a good thing, and you should continue to ask nothing of them. Influential people get asked daily for favours and advice and to have conversations with others who are looking to gain from their knowledge. They are quite accustomed to being approached and are familiar enough to know when people want something from them. Because of this, it can be hard for influencers to identify who is trustworthy in their lives, and they often are reserved because of this.

Think about an influencer you have in your life that would be a good person for you to spend more time with. Think about your relationship with that person as it exists now. Can it be made stronger in some way? When was the last time you met with this person face to face? Have you ever been alone with this person long enough to have a business or personal conversation? Make sure that you don't present yourself as just another person who wants something from them, because you may be kept at an arm's length if this is the case. Instead, ask if you can buy this person a coffee or some breakfast in exchange for conversation. Think about how you can help them. For example, if they write for a blog or post on Twitter, offer meaningful conversation in response to what they are writing about. Many successful people write about what is happening in their lives on their blogs. Learn about what is important to them.

Most people are pretty accessible these days via email, social media, and telephone. Picking up the phone is always a good option. You can just call to catch up and say hello if you already know this person. If they are more of an acquaintance or business contact, then you will have to have a reason to contact them beyond just checking in to see how they are. Perhaps ask them if they have a few minutes for you to ask them some questions about their area of expertise. Try to learn as much as you can from this person by observing what makes them successful and engaging in meaningful conversations. How do they handle stress and conflict? What have they done specifically to make them successful? What have they done that you would like to do? Each time you interact with this person, use it as an opportunity to learn and grow. Don't be afraid to ask questions about their experiences. Most successful executives are happy to share their personal experiences if they think it will help you in some way. Let's face it: we all love to talk about ourselves. Just make sure that you respect the relationship with this person and respect their time.

Once you have spent enough time talking to this person to get a sense of what their life is like, figure out if there is something you can do to help them. Even if you can't think of anything immediately, offer your help on a project, goal, or business that they are working on. Let them know that you are there for them if they need you. This demonstrates that you are not somebody who is all take and no give. You will immediately stand out from the lineup of takers around the corner who are all waiting to get five minutes alone with this person so that they can ask for a favour. View your influential friend as someone you can learn from, not take from. This person is not going to be your next big break; you, my friend, have to accomplish that all on your own. But if you play your hand right, you may just get lucky enough to have this person want to help you.

The best way for this to happen is to nurture the relationship naturally with an influential person that you really want to be friends with and resist the urge to ask them for anything. Often, you can just tell them what you are up to, and they will be intuitive enough to offer their help if they think there is something they can offer you. Influencers are very good networkers and will often say things like, *"I should put you in touch with ____ because he can probably really help you on this."* Introductions are golden when they come from influencers. Just relax and nurture the relationship first; if they can help you, trust that they will. You never want to be that friend who goes around asking for favours from anyone and everyone. You do, of course, have to ask for what you want in life and be willing to ask *of* people, but do this with the people you don't know intimately. That way, if it's a no you get back, it doesn't damage the relationship.

When you ask an influential friend for help, it puts them in an awkward position if they either can't help or don't want to. You risk straining the relationship and losing out on the benefits of being friends with such a person. Instead, keep your asks to people outside of your inner circle. Go big with those. Think pie in the sky and reach out to people. There is never harm in asking, and when it's someone you don't know that you're asking for help, you won't be hurt, and neither will they. If the answer is no, you will just move on with your life and so will they.

THE MOST IMPORTANT FINANCIAL RELATIONSHIP

Many are shocked when we tell them that the most important financial relationship they have is the one they share with their spouse. This is very true. We are very lucky to have a great relationship: we share everything, and have always had common goals. We always talked about what we wanted for ourselves from an early age, and whenever there were big decisions to make that could potentially affect the financial livelihood of the family, we always discussed it first. We have been each other's rocks and biggest supporters. But not everyone thinks like this. We have also seen men shut their wives out of financial decision-making and keep them in the dark about how bad things are financially in the household. And we have seen women hiding money from their husbands because they don't know the status of their family's finances and they worry.

The key problem in both of these examples is that there is no communication, and there just has to be. Both partners have to be on board with the family financial plan. It doesn't matter if only one is bringing in an income or if there is plenty of money. Aligning your financial goals is so important for the future of your family's finances and for the success of your future. If you are working toward a plan that your wife knows nothing about, how can she support you, and vice versa? Keep an open dialogue about what you want, how to get there, and what you think needs to happen. Share in the family budget-planning too. No one likes to talk about finances, but you simply have to. There is no getting around it. That mortgage bill will be there every month, and so will the utility bills. That won't change, so why not get comfortable with that fact, and get comfortable talking about it with your spouse?

When you and your spouse are on the same page and working toward the same goals, you make it so much easier to manifest the things that you have always wanted. You will notice that money flows in with ease, bills get paid, progress is made, and you confidently move in the direction of your dreams. This happens because your views and goals are in alignment with each other, so you create a powerful point of attraction in which you make the manifestation of your goals possible. When there is discord or silence in a relationship, each partner creates their own views about what the other is thinking and doing, and each partner operates separately in accordance with their own rules and desires. How can you accomplish the same goal when this is happening?! It will never happen, and the relationship will likely break down due to lack of trust and intimacy. Having a strong relationship in which you can speak openly and freely about things is paramount to how successful you will be in business and in life. You can't tackle the whole world on your own; you need allies by your side. And who better to stand by your side than the very person you chose to spend your life with?

KEEPING EMOTION OUT OF IT!

Money matters have been the cause of many a relationship breakdown. This has happened with marriages, with friendships, in families, and in business relationships. Emotions can wreak havoc on financial decisions and discussions. The best investors know that emotion has to stay out of financial decisions, and you simply have to remain calm and make the best decisions that will yield the best results. Part of the job of a (good) financial advisor is to manage client's emotions. When clients are investing and watching the market fluctuate, their emotions can become as volatile as the market, leading them to make poor decisions to scrap carefully thought-out long-term investment strategies that their advisors have put in place for them just so they can feel better in the short term.

The problem with this is that they are seeking short-term emotional relief and sacrificing the long-term financial benefit that they would have seen had they just kept their emotions in check and allowed the advisor to do their job. Emotions can derail us if we're not careful, and this is especially the case when money is involved. We can all think of at least a handful of people who had relationships end or break down due to financial disagreements or problems. Friends lend other friends money and repayment terms are loose; business partnerships fail when one person is irresponsible or the business fails to be profitable; a family member extends a loan that is never repaid; a spouse has a bad spending habit. There are dozens of scenarios in which relationships are under tremendous amounts of stress every day, all because of the same thing – money and emotion.

Money is transactional; it is earned, spent, saved, and given at all points throughout the day, every day. We must become comfortable with this idea first, and not get too attached to hoarding or keeping money, or we will never be bold enough to take a risk that could yield us incredible results. If you live in fear of losing your money and that is your predominant thought, there is a good chance that your predominant thought will occur. We often get what we think about most. It is important to keep emotion out of our financial relationships and discussions. Think of money in terms of practicality and logic. Remove your personal feelings and your ego and deal in straight facts and numbers. This is how you will find success in your financial relationships. If you are entering into a business relationship with a family member or a friend – or borrowing money – be as professional as you would with a bank. Create documentation for everyone to sign, draft a repayment schedule, demonstrate your assets, and outline how long you anticipate requiring the loan.

If you want a friend or a family member to invest in a business idea you have, don't pitch them the idea after you've had a few drinks. Set up a meeting to discuss the opportunity during the daytime. Have a plan drawn up. Show your friend the figures, how much you need to start up, when you expect to see profit, what you are looking for from your investors, and what you are prepared to give back in return. It doesn't matter if you are pitching your friend from elementary school – be professional and remove the element of emotion. Deal in what is, not in what was or what will be. You must lay the facts on the table as they are now, today, right now. You can talk about your projection goals and what your plan is, but you must be willing to talk about what your position is today, at this very moment.

This one is difficult, because we are so emotionally invested in our partners, but we also must do our best to keep emotion out of our marital financial discussions. Pointing the finger at each other for spending or not being diligent with bills isn't going to lead anywhere positive, and will only shut down the progress of open communication. Stick to the facts as they are. Resist the urge to judge, criticize, defend, or speak through the ego. Instead, keep conversations calm and rational, and take a collaborative approach with your partner. If you notice a financial conversation getting heated, be the one to calm it down by asking to take a tea or a coffee break. Never raise your voice or amplify the situation if your partner becomes agitated. Instead, do what you can to disarm the aggression by not feeding into it. If your partner sees you taking a proactive and calm approach to discussing the family finances, they will feel silly being the only one at the freak-out show. Eventually, they will be as calm as you are, and you can make some progress. It is important to remember that the root cause of almost all heated financial discussions is fear. This is especially true in marital conversations about money.

Angry conversations about paying bills on time, dipping into savings, quitting a job, or borrowing money are almost always related to the fear of losing everything. It is a very real fear that many people have. Our lives operate like a machine: we feed money into the machine and things keep going. Our bills get paid; we have a roof over our head; the kids get what they need; and we can continue to get from point A to point B as long as we are feeding into the machine. But what happens when the machine is broken? When one spouse loses a job or gets fired? What happens when the marriage breaks down, and it is no longer a dual-income household? What happens when someone gets sick and can no longer work to pay bills? These things do happen, and you don't want to find yourself in these situations acting out of fear and irrational emotion when you can plan for them now.

You can eliminate so much stress from your relationship simply by planning for future unexpected events and putting money aside. Saving 10 percent of your income each month will be such a relief and peace of mind for both you and your partner that your conversations about money and finances will change. You will be able to remove the emotion out of the conversations a lot easier than you can when you are operating from fear. Take the time to plan your moves so that you can approach them with a clear head instead of a desperate plan of attack. Your marriage will be so much stronger just by taking the time to set some goals and work towards them jointly. Saving and putting money aside each month is paramount to ensuring that your future marital conversations around money are less heated and more productive. It is never too late to start planning.

SPIRITUAL GUIDANCE

Whether you are religious or not, we all need some spiritual guidance from time to time to keep our mind, body, and spirit in balance. We live in a world where things move quickly, stressors occur daily, and we are under continual pressure to earn money, be a good parent, take care of our health, and be well balanced. This can be incredibly difficult when one part of your life is out of balance. If you are under financial pressure, struggling to make ends meet, the last thing on your mind is probably how you can be healthier. But all of the moving parts are interconnected and related, and a spiritual advisor, mentor, coach, or pastor can help you see this. We all need someone to talk to and what better person than someone who can help us view things from a more spiritual vantage point?

Knights of Columbus, Spiritual Mentors,
left to right, Joe, Dave Rogerson, and Mike Petis (2014)

Often, we get so wrapped up in the stressors of daily life that we forget to breathe and connect with our inner being. We forget that there is a divine person inside of us just waiting to be acknowledged, because our ego is so busy out there doing the hustle that we lose sight of the most important things. Having someone spiritual to speak to about our lives ensures that we don't lose sight of what's important and that we keep a pulse on our heart, spirit, and family. These are the most important things. If you strip away your job title, your possessions, your financial status, what are you left with? This is what needs to be nurtured. What's interesting is that when you nurture these things, the success in your material life will mirror the success in your spiritual life. Having a spiritual mentor or advisor to talk to will help you tremendously with your spiritual growth. It doesn't matter what your personal beliefs are or what religion you practice, we all have people in our community who can help us connect to the spirit that lives within. If that is missing in your life, go to church one Sunday morning and see how it feels, or seek out a meditation group or a spiritual interest group to connect with. Taking the time to nurture your spirituality will help every facet of your life, but most importantly, your relationships.

Many spiritual groups and churches get involved in community activities such as fundraisers, charities, and community causes. Joining a local church or spiritual group is a great way to get involved in what's happening in your community and give you the opportunity to develop meaningful relationships with people that are built on mutual trust, generosity, and concern for the well-being of others. These are strong foundations from which to form relationships. The more involved in your community you are and the more that you give back, the happier you will be as a person. It's interesting how happiness is directly tied to giving, not receiving. Being generous with your time, money, effort, or anything else you have to offer is a wonderful feeling, whereas receiving feels good for a short amount of time and then fades until you eventually want something else. You can never quite fill that void when you are constantly in want. But giving is a gift that extends far beyond the act itself. It releases stress and anxiety, creates meaningful relationships, makes us happy, and makes us feel connected to the world at large by making us feel that we are a part of something much bigger than ourselves. We urge you to get out there into your community and offer yourself to local charities, causes, churches, and advocacy groups. Just try it for a month or two and notice how great you feel inside. And when you feel great inside, it shows on the outside, in all that you do and all that you are.

GINA'S ADVICE FOR COUPLES

Communication in a marriage is key. Talking about finances openly and honestly is so important to your relationship's overall health. I've encountered so many situations where a husband or wife had a debt that they didn't want the other to know about. One of them will call me and tell me to omit the debt from the conversation, making things very uncomfortable for me, because now, I'm in the awkward position of being caught in the middle of a situation that could explode at any time.

Back in 2017, I had a client that came to me – a professional woman with a good job and a strong, reliable income. She and her husband had their mortgage paid off and owned their home, which was impressive. Her husband was more of a saver in the relationship and controlled her spending as well as his own. She called me in a panic because she had secretly racked up $70,000 of debt and was starting to have problems making the payments. She had the statements going to another address, and the husband had no idea. We eventually had no choice but to bring her husband into the discussion, as we realized the only way to deal with the debt appropriately was to put a mortgage on the house to pay it off. Soon after this incident, the couple unfortunately separated. The deception and lack of communication deteriorated the trust in the relationship. This is just one of many stories that we encounter every day in working with couples.

TIPS FOR SUCCESS:

- *Don't keep anything a secret from each other, because it eventually comes out and makes issues much worse. It also makes rebuilding trust very difficult.*
- *Have long-term and short-term money goals that you are both aligned on. A goal could be taking a vacation, buying a new home or a cottage, renovating your kitchen, or buying a new car. Whatever the goal is, plan together and strategize how to make the plan into a reality.*
- *Always have a budget. This is a living, breathing, and constantly evolving document that you should refer to frequently. Identify how much you are*

spending and where to determine how you can improve in order to achieve your financial goals.

- Set up a savings account and try to put a percentage of your income into that account weekly, biweekly, or monthly, depending on when you get paid.

Always celebrate when you've reached a goal or milestone in your finances.

Renewing our vows on our 25th Wedding Anniversary, with Father Dan Hinsperger at St. Luke's Church (2015)

JOE'S ADVICE FOR COUPLES

When I am giving couples advice about budgeting and finances, I always ask them how many accounts they have. It's very interesting to see the array of different perspectives and relationships we encounter when it comes to finance. Most young couples we see have three accounts; her account, his account, and the couple's combined account. They run their life together as a business. This may work for some couples, but I am an advocate for trust, transparency, and teamwork in a relationship, and this often lends itself to individualistic thinking. Because of this, I believe that having one joint account for all expenses and a joint savings account is the best way forward to achieve shared financial goals in a relationship. I know some couples may disagree with this or think that it's outdated thinking, but it really comes down to compete and total honesty. There is nothing to hide when everything is out in the open.

Aligning your financial and personal goals with your spouse's is the most important aspect of your relationship. Unity will lead to longevity and a healthier happier relationship. Each partner can always budget for miscellaneous or personal expenses for the week that can be discretionary. The key is just to put it in the budget, agree on what that number is, and ensure that your shared monthly budget aligns with your financial goals as a couple. Relationships cannot be conditional on financial matters. There's a lot more to a relationship than simply managing finances together, and it really begins with trust and communication. Managing your joint finances should be secondary to the crucial foundation of trust and communication in your relationship, which always comes first.

I remember working with an older couple who had been married for many years, and they had separate bank accounts and separate credit card accounts. The home and paying off the mortgage was mostly where the husband focused his attention – he wanted to pay off the mortgage as quickly as possible. Their combined annual income was equal to the mortgage amount. So, paying off the mortgage quickly was a realistic goal for the couple to achieve based purely on the numbers. Until she disclosed a credit card that had the same balance as the mortgage. The card was also at an incredibly high interest rate of 19 percent. Truth and transparency was lacking in this relationship, to say the least. I recommended to the couple that they sit down together to discuss indebtedness and share with each other all outstanding debts that hadn't yet been disclosed. Within a week I was called and asked to proceed with the new mortgage to pay out the credit card. Unfortunately, the marriage did not last. Although they had managed to stay together for many years with their separate finances, this massive, secret debt was ultimately the nail in the coffin for this couple.

HEALTH

Anyone who doesn't see the direct connection between health and money is perhaps not looking close enough. These two things, which some may say have nothing to do with each other, are in fact very closely connected. One of the biggest external factors that influence our overall health and wellness is the state of our finances. If we are plagued by debt, have collectors calling us, and can't seem to pay our bills on time, then stress and anxiety are likely prevalent in our lives. Stress causes a whole host of illnesses and medical complications, and there is nothing more stressful than not being able to pay our bills. In order to both survive and thrive in our society, we simply have to have the income to support our financial lives. If we live beyond our means, then we are setting ourselves up for failure. But when we live within our means, making payments and keeping on top of things becomes much easier and less stressful. The less stressful our financial interactions, the more peaceful we feel inside.

Sometimes, however, we are hit with unexpected financial hardship, and this can create an incredible amount of stress, especially when it is something we didn't see coming. It can really rock our foundation to the core and cause us to slip into a depressive state of mind. We have to consciously be aware of our emotional health when dealing with financial matters, because the energy that these interactions create sets the stage for what our financial future looks like. We are continually paving the path of the future with our thoughts, feelings, and attitudes about things, including money. For this reason, having a firm grasp on our emotions and our overall health is a really important factor in manifesting abundance in our lives. You cannot attract prosperity when you come from a position of lack or "not enough." You have to be living in the light of abundance to be able to attract it, which doesn't always come easy if you are having trouble making ends meet. The trick, though (as we will discuss later), is to notice abundance in every area, not just the balance of your bank account.

HOW STRESS IMPACTS YOUR HEALTH

Think about how you feel when you encounter a stressful situation or are dealing with a high degree of stress. You, like many others, are probably well-equipped to see the warning signs of stress and have a familiarity with it. But there are so many areas of our health that stress can impact that we often don't think about. There are, of course, many physical indicators, from nausea to heart palpitations, sweaty palms, diarrhea, headaches, lethargy, and aches and pains. But if all of that is happening on the outside of the body, then what is happening on the inside? The answer is *a lot*. In fact, stress affects almost every area of your body and can wreak havoc on the normal functioning of almost everything, from your digestive system to your central nervous system. Many people don't think about the impact of stress on their bodies and are more concerned with the actual stressor than the continuing, long-term effects of stress. But this is a big problem area that we all need to focus on to ensure that we are doing everything we can to eliminate or reduce the stress in our lives and change the way we react to external circumstances that are out of our control.

Stress can weaken your immune system, making you more susceptible to colds and viruses; it can shorten your menstrual cycles or stop your periods all together; it can give you heartburn and ulcers and be the cause of IBS (Irritable Bowel Syndrome); it can create respiratory challenges; and it can increase your risk for heart attack and stroke. These are just a few of the health impacts of stress, and there are, unfortunately, many more. Additionally, almost every illness or disease can be worsened by the presence of stress in the body. Reducing or eliminating stress in your life has never been more important for your body. Stress also creates a number of emotional and behavioural effects in addition to the physical symptoms. Some of us binge eat when we are under stress, looking to comfort ourselves through food. This just makes us feel worse in the end, with the increase in pounds that we see on the scale a few days later. Others prefer to indulge in vices such as alcohol or drugs when they are stressed out, which is essentially just issue avoidance. The impact of alcohol and drugs can often be much more severe than stress, and still doesn't get to the heart of the matter or make you face your challenge head on.

Substance abuse problems have long been blamed on stressful life circumstances, but escapism does little to change the situation, and in fact, almost always make things worse. Other side effects of stress include anger, irritability, negativity, hopelessness, depression, and even suicide. Some people feel so desperate that they see no way out. Never underestimate the power of stress on the human body and mind, and never assume that it is just something that someone can snap out of, either. In order to be less affected by stress, it requires some practice and a re-training of the brain. This is difficult for some, especially if they have always relied on the comfort of negative thinking and cynicism. Changing behaviours can be scary, even if doing so means a better life. It is the same reason why the alcoholic can't give up the bottle. They know that it isn't good for them, that it is harming their relationships with family and wreaking havoc on their health, but they fear change. Some people are perpetually in a state of chaos and stress. Sure, they don't like it, and the toll it has taken on them is likely very obvious to others, but they fear what not living like that would look like. If you don't know what's on the other side of the fence, it can seem scary or even intimidating. And sometimes, people fear living up to responsibility or even fear their own success.

WHEN STRESS IS A PROBLEM

We are human beings, so none of us are going to be completely free of stress, but we can certainly reduce the amount of stress in our lives by making better choices, controlling our thoughts and emotions, and treating our body in a positive way. Stress does become a problem, however, if it is prolonged or it becomes a way of life. Some of us are so accustomed to living a life of stress that we may not even notice just how stressful things are. When stress is a prolonged daily occurrence, it is time to consider alternate ways of managing your life. You can usually tell when it is a problem because things just seem to be crumbling around you. Perhaps your relationships are struggling, you feel angry and irritated all the time, you resent your job or your boss, you feel awful about the way you look, and you think negatively most of the time – making very little room for optimism. It is very important for you to recognize when you are in this state of mind, because unless you want to continue to live like this, it is imperative that you change. Most negative people aren't that way because they enjoy it, they are that way because they have given up on being positive. If they were to tell you why, it would probably be something like, *"I just can't get ahead no matter what I do, so what's the point?"* They have become jaded by their experiences. It might have started with a couple of unlucky circumstances, but then those random circumstances formed into limiting beliefs – and that is where the danger is.

We cannot protect ourselves from unexpected external life circumstances. We weren't prepared to have a son die, nor was our family prepared to face the fear and uncertainty a cancer diagnosis. But both things happened. We could either take those life situations and let them form into limiting beliefs about how unlucky we are or how unfair life is, or we can view them for what they are – uncontrollable and unpredictable life circumstances. The danger with feeling unlucky, that life is unfair, or that you just can't get ahead is that you will be unable to see anything positive when you come from that angle. You will be so focused on the negative things that happen to you that you will miss all the positives. The age-old glass is half-empty versus half-full analogy. How you view the world and the things that happen to you is entirely up to you, but one way leads to far greater success and happiness, and I am sure you can guess which way that is.

When you come from a negative point of view and are unhappy about your life, you actually continue to attract further negative circumstances into your life. The law of attraction states that your thoughts, actions, and emotions will attract to you the essence of what you focus on. If this isn't a motivator for you to quickly seek stress relief, then I don't know what is. Thinking negatively attracts more negativity. Believing that you are unlucky will turn into a self-fulfilling prophecy of unlucky events, and being angry or irritated will provide you with an abundance of opportunity to further be angry and irritated about other things in your life. You simply cannot afford to waste your time focusing on stress and negativity. It is imperative (for your own sake) that you change the energy of your thoughts and attitude before you attract more of the same energy.

HOW TO REDUCE THE STRESS IN YOUR LIFE

If you are like most, you wake up in the mornings, rush to get ready for work, head out the door, and fight rush-hour traffic both there and back. Perhaps you have a stressful job, or you work long hours, or you never have time to eat properly, so you eat your lunch out every day. All of these things are warning signs and could potentially lead you down the wrong path. It is OK to work long hours when you are loving what you are doing, and it is OK if you have a stressful job if you are good at managing the stress, and it is even OK to eat out every day if you are making wise choices – but unfortunately, these things rarely ring true for the average office worker trying to make ends meet and providing for a family. The pressures of earning an income, raising a family, and paying bills can feel insurmountable at times, but with effective stress management techniques, you can alleviate the symptoms of stress.

Reducing stress in your life means that you are going to have to change it up and potentially do something different, that you may not have done before. You are going to have to change, which is a scary word for some. But the main reason this will benefit you is that you will now be in a position to see opportunities, manifest abundance, and experience greater success. When you are in a stressed out, negative state of mind, you are in the wrong energy to succeed. By contrast, when you are relaxed, optimistic, and feeling good, anything is possible. There are some wonderful techniques and lifestyle changes that you can make right now to improve your life and reduce the amount of stress you feel.

MEDITATION

Meditation is not just for yoga enthusiasts, new-age types, or people backpacking through Nepal. Mediation is a tool that you can use in your everyday life to connect with your own sense of inner peace. The cause of human suffering is our attachment to past- and future-based thinking. The mind is a busy place, with millions of thoughts passing through it each day. Think of the mind as a highway and the thoughts as cars. Some of them might travel with you for a while, and others will just be a short distance thought. Not all of our thoughts are meaningful and valid, and in fact, many are not. Meditation helps us get away from the everyday stress of thinking by allowing us to just float in our existence and be peaceful, without thoughts. The goal of meditation is to not think, and to gently push thoughts away with your mind when they try to come into your meditation practice. You can meditate at work, on the bus, lying in bed, or sitting on the couch or outside under a tree. You don't have to make a big deal out of it. Just spend a few minutes per day with your eyes closed, resisting the urge to think. Let your breath be your guide, and allow yourself to just be you, without all of the incessant rambling and chatter that goes on in your mind. Breathe in deeply and exhale slowly a few times until you feel as if you are just floating.

Don't judge yourself if you do have thoughts that attempt to interrupt your practice, just gently push them away from you and visualize them dissipating into the clouds. Use your breath as something to focus on if your thoughts continue to harass you. Doing this for only ten or fifteen minutes in the morning before you start your day can drastically change the energy of your day for the better. You will be calmer, happier, and better equipped to handle challenges. Meditation has hundreds of benefits and no known negative effects, so that alone should be enough reason to try.

STAYING PRESENT

We never focus on the present moment because we are always too busy thinking about something that has already happened, or fantasizing about something that hasn't yet happened and might never happen. Imagine you made a huge mistake at work that cost the company thousands of dollars. You go home and cannot stop thinking about it. You obsess over it, tell your husband or wife, do some stress eating, and basically think about it all night. The next day, your boss is nowhere to be found so you start imagining that he is in a meeting discussing your mistake and how to fire you. You build up this whole fantasy event inside of your head and are convinced that you will be fired. You don't see your boss for three days because he is in and out of meetings, and the entire time, you stress, worry, and feel sick to your stomach about what you feel is your inevitable demise. Eventually, your boss comes by your office, asks how you are doing, and smiles at you. He doesn't even mention the mistake. This causes you to rethink everything. Was your mistake perhaps not that big of a deal? This type of thinking occurs on a daily basis and is part of the human condition.

We cannot change the things that have already happened, so why give them any more thought? They have already happened and are unchangeable. We can only choose to change right now, in this moment of life, because it is all that we are guaranteed. You don't know if you are going to get a tomorrow, but you have a today, so why not deal with that right now? Don't waste your precious time thinking about something that has already happened, or something that might never happen. What a waste of your vital life force.

When you stay present, life really isn't that stressful, because you know that you can handle whatever is happening, because you are. It is only when you start jumping into the future with your fear-based thinking that things get stressful. Resist the urge to create fantasies about what might, could, or will happen. You don't know the outcome, and stressing about any situation will only attract negative energy to the situation at hand. Instead, focus on right now. What can you do right now to make things better for tomorrow? Stay present with your work, thoughts, and activities and keep them in the now. You will find this much more peaceful and helpful.

EXERCISE

This is the part where everyone groans, "Oh no, not exercise!" But once you get into a groove with exercise, it will feel so good that you will be unwilling to go without it. The trick is to find something that you enjoy. If you are not a gym person and hate the gym, don't get another membership thinking this time, things will be different – try something else. You can join sports teams, do yoga in your home, go running, or ride your bike every day. There are so many activities for you to get involved in and no shortage of people in your city or town doing them. Incorporating exercise into your life has tremendous health benefits that reach far beyond the physical. You will experience an increase in confidence, feel more balanced, and release endorphins, which are your feel-good receptors. Basically, exercising regularly will make you feel awesome. Finding the motivation to exercise when you are in a negative or stressful state of mind can be a catch-twenty-two sometimes. You know that exercising will make you feel better, yet you don't have the motivation to want to, even though you know it will help. For this reason, it is so important to find something that you actually enjoy doing. In the winter, maybe it is snowboarding, ice skating, or taking your kids tobogganing, and then in the summer, maybe it's rowing or downhill mountain biking. If you aren't sure what you like, just start trying things. Guaranteed, you will find something that you can get into.

The reason why so many people give up on their gym memberships is because they haven't considered that maybe they just aren't "gym people." Some people are just bored to tears on the treadmill and wandering around the free weights. Others really just don't feel comfortable in that type of environment. It doesn't matter what your reason is. Just start trying other types of exercise. Anything that gets you up off the couch and out of the house is a good thing – especially if you are experiencing a lot of stress. Exercise keeps you present with what you are doing (which reduces stress), and it releases endorphins that make you feel happy. Getting physical exercise makes you feel great about yourself and less stressed about whatever is troubling you that day. It presses the reset button and enables you to be in a different state of mind that is far more productive and opportunistic.

Orange Theory, 2022

HEALTHY EATING

Have you noticed that the foods you eat have their own vibrational frequency? It's true. Think about the way you feel after you eat a combo meal from a drive-thru restaurant. Now think about the way you feel after you eat a healthy, home cooked meal at a family member's house. The two are completely different. Fast food and restaurant-prepared food are often severely unhealthy. They use a lot of butters and fats, and you are likely overdosing on carbohydrates, which make you feel tired and sluggish and interfere with your brain functions. Carbohydrates from breads, pastas, cereals, and grains convert into sugar inside of your body, which spikes your glycemic index. This is why you often feel tired after you eat: you are not getting sufficient energy from your food. Carbohydrates are also very addictive, often sending you searching for food every two hours. It's always the carb foods that we have the most trouble giving up, and they are the most troubling to our bodies. Thankfully, you can eat more proteins, like eggs, meat, and fish, as well as vegetables, and they will not make you feel like that. In fact, eating more vegetables and proteins and limiting your carbohydrate intake is probably one of the best things you can do to feel better during the day and energize yourself.

You will also notice that you lose weight and that your brain seems quicker and more alert. I don't want to sit here and give you diet advice about this diet or that diet, because we all have our own preferences and techniques and there are a lot of schools of thought about what works and what doesn't. But you should at least be willing to look at your daily food intake and form an opinion about how healthfully you are eating. Are you eating a lot of fresh vegetables? Are you limiting your sugars and carbohydrates? Are you choosing the healthiest methods for preparing your foods (for example, steaming, poaching, baking)? There are some great tools both online and for your mobile device that can help you track your food, count your calories, and show you which foods you should be eating. Healthy eating will boost your confidence, make your eyes and skin glow, and boost your immune system. Additionally, you feel happier when you eat better, because of the high vibration of the foods you are eating. Packaged foods or foods prepared in fast-food restaurants are low-vibration foods because they don't originate in nature and are often created by humans in a laboratory. The food that will have you feeling the best is the food that you eat in its most natural state.

Things that grow and come from the earth and don't require much altering: salads, root vegetables, greens, and herbs. Try incorporating more healthy natural foods into your diet and notice how much better you feel.

AVOIDING FINANCIAL STRESS

Financial stress seems almost unavoidable. Where there is money, there is passion, and where there is lack, there is stress. We cannot avoid the fact that we live in a society where money matters. Having too much can create paranoia about losing it, being ripped off, being robbed, or becoming a target. Having too little can create desperation, stress, and health problems when bills don't get paid and there isn't enough money to pay for day-to-day things. But like many things in our lives, money is energy, and the attitude we have about money creates the energy we project. If we are in position of paranoia about being taken advantage of, it is very probable that we may end up continually experiencing this, simply because we focus on that. Just like if we are focusing on a lack of cash flow, we will continue to experience a lack of cash flow. It sounds simple because it is simple. We cannot project negative energy about financial situations and expect positive outcomes. Instead, we have to change the story inside of our heads so that it sounds better than what we've been telling ourselves – and not only do we have to change the story, but we have to believe it.

We have to know that whatever financial hardship or challenge we are facing is temporary and will pass, because all things are temporary. Nothing is permanent. If we lose money in a deal, make a bad investment, or lend money to somebody who doesn't pay it back, there is nothing we can do to change those events once they have already happened. Accept what is (including being ripped off, not being able to pay your bills, or making a bad investment) and deal with the reality of the situation. But know that it isn't going to be like this forever. The energy of money is fast and is always moving. Don't allow yourself to get trapped in an inflexible state of mind about something that has already happened. Just roll with the punches and know that tomorrow is another day. If you can't seem to stop obsessing over a financial stressor, then do whatever you have to in order to change the energy of your thoughts. Go visit a friend, head out for a bike ride, do some meditation or yoga, or spend time with family. Change your state of mind by doing something that you know will put you in a better state of mind.

Obsessing on negative thoughts is dangerous, especially when it comes to your finances. Accept the situation and move on. Things will inevitably change and will look different next week than they do right now, and even more different in a year from now. Ask yourself, "Will this matter to me a year from now?" If the answer is no, then don't continue to obsess and stress over it. Snap yourself into a better frame of mind by focusing on the good and seeing the glass as half-full.

BE PROACTIVE WITH YOUR HEALTH

There is only one you, and only one body, so it is important to treat it well. You cannot clone yourself into a faster, better, leaner version of yourself. What you are is what you have, so you must work with that. You can choose to make poor decisions and pay for them later, or you can choose to make good decisions now that will benefit you later. Unhealthy eating, sedentary living, and substance abuse are things that all catch up with you eventually. It may not be today or tomorrow or next week, but eventually, you will have a price to pay for your continued neglect in these areas. The good news is that you have the ability and chance to change and reverse all of this right now by being proactive with your health. Don't wait for a doctor to put you on heart medication or antidepressants or diagnose you with diabetes. Change begins with you, and you can choose to change today.

The choices you make impact your family, your children, and your friends. You shouldn't be willing to do anything to your body that is potentially damaging or fatal. If you know that you are eating awfully, then start making changes to your diet. If you know that you aren't getting enough exercise, start integrating it into your lifestyle. If you know that you are a bit of a hothead, begin introducing meditation to your life. We all have warning signs and whispers from the universe telling us that we are either on the right track or we need to make changes. Follow the breadcrumb trail and be proactive about your health. Don't wait until you are forced to change when you can experience a great quality of life right now.

GINA'S REFLECTIONS ON HEALTH

Our habits help define who we are as human beings, and we develop many habits over time for different facets of our lives – in health, finance, relationships, and more. Our sense of discipline and commitment is what ultimately helps turn a plan into a habit. One thing that is very important to me is exercising three or four times per week, because I know it is beneficial to my physical, mental and emotional health. This has developed into a healthy habit because I prioritized it in my life and committed to making it a part of my routine. I choose a consistent time every day and I show up for myself. This is non-negotiable for me, it sets my mood and attitude for the day and improves my mental clarity. There is a saying that "an ounce of prevention is worth a pound of cure", and another that says health is wealth. I wholeheartedly believe these statements and have directly experienced the positive impact that exercise has had upon my health in every way. You have to take the time to care for yourself first before you can effectively take care of others, and before you can take care of business.

Another important ritual for me pertains to family dinners. It has always been important that we eat together at the end of the day and share conversation. From the time the kids were young into adulthood, we have had dinner together. It is expected, and if they cannot make it, they let me know. Having dinner together allows us to connect and have conversations about the day and helps to create a stronger family bond that supports all of our health and well-being. I enjoy cooking and making healthy food for my family, since the foods we consume daily have an enormous impact on our health. I always plan out our family meals for the week and have always done this since having children. Having our sons join us in our business did not happen overnight – many of these conversations about their futures and roles in our business were had over family dinners. Even at a young age, they would get to hear about our day at work and any challenges we were having, which molded them into the young men they are today.

Joe and I have always tried to create and promote a healthy environment for our children, which includes spiritual, physical, mental, and emotional well-being.

When the kids were growing up, we had the same routine on Sundays: get up, breakfast, and then off to church – and this would be followed by Sunday lunch with our own family or extended family and grandparents. This was similar to my own upbringing as a child with my family. My parents came from a very devout Catholic family, my aunt being a mother superior in Rome.

We encouraged the kids to be involved with the church because we knew it supported their overall health and wellbeing. They were altar boys, Joe was a Eucharistic minister, and I was a word minister. It was important for us to have the kids involved in our church community. Although it was an effort at times to get everyone to church, it was worth it. I think it was important for us to plant those seeds, which would build the foundation for a responsible, faith-filled life for our children and hopefully, one day, their own children. It has also been our faith that has guided Joe and I through the worst times of our lives, and we know that it will help us with any challenges in life as we continue to move forward.

Modeling this behavior to our sons and being involved in the church is an important aspect. You can't just say something and then do the opposite. Our sons model this Christian behavior, they have organized fundraising events for causes that are close to their hearts and are all involved in the Knights of Columbus. They probably don't attend church as often as I would like them to, but they show their faith every day in how they treat and care for others and the respect that they show. This is more important than money or wealth. They understand that being materialistic will result in becoming spiritually broke, because allowing money to come in between you and your faith will result in unethical behaviour.

This is what we preach to them, and I'm proud of the young men they have become.

left to right, Nicole, Thomas, Joe with Valentina, Gina with Isabella, Matthew, and Daniel, on our 30th Wedding Anniversary, (2020)

Ultimately, your mindset is what will help to lay the foundation that you need in your life to have healthy habits and rituals that will lead you to a healthier life. Mindset is incredibly important and supports healthy relationships with others and the formation of healthy habits and activities that are good for your mental health. I have come to realize over time that most successful people are passionate about what they do and are rarely influenced by negativity. They are always learning and have the ability to overcome negative people and events. They don't go back and dwell on mistakes, they fix them. So, I always do my best to maintain a positive outlook, even in the face of adversity. There is always something that can be taken away from a challenging situation. It's just how we frame it in our minds that matters.

left to right, Isabella, Natalia, Valentina (December 2022)

I love my job, so working long hours has never really bothered me. The days go by quickly because of how busy I am. But though I am creating wealth for my family, it does take a toll on my health. Much of my day is spent sitting, so I'm very inactive for long periods of time. Taking calls, trying to get deals underwritten and approved, and having deadlines creates a lot of stress, which gets harder to handle as you get older.

I started making more serious life changes in my forties. I knew if I continued on without making lifestyle changes, that could lead me down the road to serious illness. I needed to devote more time to myself, that included walking to combat the number of hours that I would be sitting, weightlifting to increase my muscle mass, healthier eating to keep my weight down and reduce inflammation in my body, trying to get better restorative sleep and meditation. This all made a huge difference to my mental health and well-being

There are a lot of things I would have done differently looking back on my life, especially when it comes to managing financial stress. I think I would tell the younger Gina, "Don't worry, you got this!" I spent too much time worrying as a younger woman, and worrying can cause such stress on the mind and body. It is an emotion that can overtake you and paralyze you from action. For me, taking control of a situation the best I can is all I can do, and if I fail, I fail – but worrying has no control over the outcome, so why worry?!

JOE'S SECRETS TO LIVE BY

There's a couple of secrets to life that I live by. One of them is about doing good and forgetting about it. I don't do things for any reason other than they simply need to be done. I don't do it for praise, or to be able to say, "look what I did," or to be able to turn around and ask for a favour in return from someone. I just don't think about it. I do good things when they need to be done, period. And yet that always seems to come back to me in some way, even though that is the last thing on my mind.

"There's an old Italian saying that goes, "the one who helps himself will end up helping three people." I believe that strongly. I am a very fortunate man, and not a day goes by when I don't acknowledge that. If I didn't focus on my own health, wealth, and success, I'd be no use to anyone. So, the thing that I had to do in my life to put me in the position I am in today was to focus relentlessly on building success for myself. Because only then was I able to utilize that success to help others, including my family."

BALANCE

So by now, you have learned about Cash Flow, Attitude, Relationships, and Health. Balance is the fifth factor, and it is perhaps the most important, because without balance in your life, you cannot make your life work in all four areas. If any of these areas is out of balance, you will notice that other things begin to suffer. For example, if your career is going amazingly well and you are making plenty of money, but are never home, perhaps your marriage is suffering, or you have no time to date if you are single. Or maybe you are so focused on working out and hitting the gym that you are ignoring other things in your life, like your relationships and work responsibilities. There are plenty of ways in which a life can become unbalanced, and the key is really to balance it all so that you can feel at peace with the flow of your life.

When your life is unbalanced, it feels stressful, whether there is money or not. Sometimes, our lack of balance in life is unintentional. We just become so focused on a goal or one particular area of our life that we unknowingly turn our back on other important things. Achieving balance in life isn't always easy, and sometimes, we face relationship problems, challenges, and life-changing circumstances before we are able to see that things are out of balance. Thankfully, by keeping our finger on the pulse of our priorities and continually taking stock of our lives, we will be able to avoid most life-balance issues simply by being conscious of balance. When we are too hyper-focused on one area of our life, it is easy to forget another, but having our sights set on all of the priorities in our lives and knowing what they are helps us manage our responsibilities in a way that ensures we don't forget about things or drop the ball. Sometimes, when we are chasing a dream, it's the ones closest to us (our spouses and children) who suffer the most, by us not spending as much time with them or being away all the time. There are certain areas of life that are of great importance to all humans, but the degree of importance will change from person to person, depending on what they are focused on at any particular time. These common areas are mind, body, spirit, finances and career, and family and social life. Or, to take it one step further, they can be defined as the following:

Mind: Learning, education, intelligence, emotional health
Body: Health, exercise, body image, active lifestyle
Spirit: Connection to a higher purpose, mediation, church, community
Finances and Career: Financial health, career, sense of purpose, success
Family and Social Life: Connection to others, family and spouse relationships

We have already talked about many of these areas in the preceding Factors and their connection to your ability to manifest financial well-being in your life. But what happens when one or more of these areas is out of balance? How do you know and what can you do about it? The Factors are only useful to you if you can balance their influence in your life. And this will be a necessity to achieve financial well-being. Sure, you might be able to be successful in one or more areas of your life even if you are unbalanced, but if you want to experience lasting success and happiness by living the Factors, you will need to learn how to balance your life appropriately in all areas.

SO, HOW DO I BALANCE MY LIFE?

First, you have to take stock of your life and assess your priorities. The best way to do this is to list everything that takes up your time. Ideally, you want to include things that are a regular part of your life and that are priorities for you. Once you have listed everything that takes up your time in the course of a week, look at which category these things fall into and label them. You can use the common areas mentioned above (mind, body, spirit, finances, social) if you would like, or create your own names for them. Look at your list after you have labeled everything and identify whether your list is balanced. Is there too much mind and finance and not enough spirit and social? Or vice versa? Spend some time really analyzing your list and being honest with yourself about where you fall balance-wise. Once you have determined which areas (if any) are out of balance, start a new list and write down five to ten things you can do to support each area that is currently out of balance. For example, if you aren't getting enough time with your friends or family, you can write down things like "Sunday family dinner," "guys" night out," or "one phone call to a friend per week."

Simply observing which area is out of balance is the first step for you to achieve balance. If we just continue on with our day to day with no visibility into what is missing in our lives, then we don't put ourselves in the position to fix anything. Aside from doing the above exercise to identify which areas are out of balance, we can usually tell when things are out of balance due to our emotional state. Your emotions serve as a wonderful gauge for how well things are going in your life. When things are going well, we tend to feel good inside, we smile more, and we feel calm, centred, and happy. But when an area of our life isn't going well, we tend to feel stressed out, angry, irritated, or depressed.

If you feel any of these negative emotions, it is very possible that your life is out of balance. If you aren't sure why and you haven't completed the exercise above, give it a try to see if you can determine why. Another thing you can do is ask yourself, "What is missing in my life?" and see what answer comes to you. Your higher self will automatically answer the question by giving you a feeling, thought, or sensation that speaks to the question. When something is missing or simply out of balance, it can cause a great deal of emotional turmoil in our lives – even ruin relationships, families, and finances. So, balancing our lives is tremendously important.

ORGANIZATION

Sometimes, when things feel out of balance in our lives, all we need is a little bit of organization and time management. Life can be stressful, and if you are trying to manage too many things at once, it is sometimes very difficult, and things start to drop. A lot of people get stressed out by the thought of paperwork-intensive tasks like taxes, government documents, or other arduous legal tasks relating to home or business. Even the process of getting a mortgage is stressful for our clients. I see them time and time, again becoming flustered by the process, but it is almost always the ones who are disorganized who are affected most. They may have forgotten some requested paperwork, or gone tearing up their homes looking for things. Sometimes, they arrive at the office with a jumbled mess of papers, with nothing in order and a nervous demeanour. I am not joking when I say that this can be fixed with about ten minutes of organization. It starts with knowing what is required. As with any submission of paperwork, supporting documents are often required, and sometimes it is work to collect those documents. So, I often tell my clients to work slowly through the process. Write a list of everything that is required, then tackle everything one by one and check it off when you have it. Put the paperwork in order as you collect it.

By the time you are finished, you will feel way more organized and will have everything you need to submit your paperwork. You can apply this list process to almost any task that requires some organization. If you are feeling overwhelmed or flustered by a set of tasks, simply take a few minutes to breathe, and then sit down and write down everything that you have to do. The act of writing a list and getting it all down on paper gives your brain a process to follow and makes the tasks appear less stressful because you aren't trying to continually remember or think about ten things simultaneously. You can focus on one thing at a time, then move on to the next thing when you have completed that. This process can be very helpful in life, whether it is at work while you are trying to accomplish your daily tasks, at home with your family, or when managing your business. Look at the areas of your life that require a bit of organization and ask yourself if you could benefit from implementing this strategy.

It is not just task-based activities that require organization – everything from how tidy our home is to our sense of time management is important. When our home is cluttered and we are perpetually looking for things, that creates unnecessary stress in our lives. Keeping a tidy space and putting things in the same place every time by creating a home for everything makes our day run smoother. We know where to find our car keys, last year's taxes, and that paper where we wrote down all of those phone numbers. We know this because we are organized, and we put things in a logical place, so we don't have to stress and worry about finding things.

Similarly, if you have a busy calendar, being organized can make your life run much smoother. Simply waking up and running out the door with no knowledge of what meetings you have that day or where the kids have to be can create a high degree of stress, especially when something takes more time or a meeting goes longer than you thought. This is also how people forget about appointments and meetings. They aren't organized and don't have a system for managing their time, so things get forgotten. Make use of your calendar, your day timer, or your phone. You can set reminders or alerts, or if you're not a technology person, just write yourself a list with all of the times and where you have to be at each time. Try to do this the night before, or early in the morning before you start your day, so that you know how your day looks before you begin.

ASSESS YOUR HAPPINESS

You can always tell when things are out of balance because you are not content. Typically, we feel angry, resentful, stressed out, or depressed when something is up. There may be an underlying feeling of doom or hopelessness. If you notice that you are feeling any of these things, it is imperative to assess why. Sometimes, balancing your life means giving up something that isn't working. This might be an unhealthy relationship, a job that makes you miserable, or a responsibility that you agreed to take on but that you don't really have time for. Whatever your issue, face it head on. Before you make a decision to give up on something entirely, make sure that the problem you are having isn't related to a simple lack of organization. If you are disorganized, it can make a task or activity feel almost unbearable, but things change drastically when you're organized, and what was once a dreaded nightmare can almost become enjoyable. You will know the difference between something that you just need to be more organized with and something that you need to give up. Trust in your intuition and if you are ever unsure, spend some time meditating on it, praying on it, or simply asking the universe.

Life is supposed to be happy and enjoyable; it isn't all work and struggle, and if it is … well, then, something's not right. You are not really living. You have to laugh, smile, feel content, and fall asleep in a hammock sometimes. If you notice your emotional state is slipping into negativity, start making changes. Do things that make you happy. Sometimes, it is that simple. Too much work and no play makes us miserable, and too much play and no work makes us stressed and feeling worthless, so balance is so very important. When we grow up, have families, and start paying bills, it doesn't mean that we can no longer have hobbies or interests or enjoy playing. Studies show that adults who have fun, laugh, and engage in fun activities live longer, feel happier, and are healthier. So, there is more value in play than just a smile and a break from your work. Play with your kids – go tobogganing, ice skating, or swimming with them. Kick a ball around outside or play catch. Those moments mean so much to a child and stay with them.

Also, make sure that you make time for yourself. If you are only focused on work, finances, and family, then your own needs may be getting left behind. What are your personal interests and hobbies? Do you nurture them? Do something once per week that is only for you. It can be drinks with a friend, attending an art class, a bowling night, or just a bike ride around the park. Whatever it is that makes you feel really good inside. Focus on that, get more of it into your life – because that matters, and it makes you whole.

ADJUSTING TO CHANGE

Some of the most challenging times in our lives are when we are faced with change. Humans are creatures of habit. We get accustomed to our routines and get into the groove of our day-to-day lifestyles. But those grooves inevitably get disrupted by any number of changes that can and will occur. Perhaps we move to a new city, we lose a job, the family separates, we get sick, or there is a death in the family. These types of things are disruptive to the normality of our lives and force us to have to live in an uncharted way. A way that isn't comfortable. But in that discomfort, there is personal growth, and that is why we simply have to welcome change into our lives and not fear it. If we just clung to our safe little corner of the world and never ventured out to try anything new, experience a different way of life, or overcome adversity, we would be ignorant to the world around us. True growth happens at the end of our comfort zone, where we don't know what's around the corner or what might happen next, but we know that we will be capable of handling whatever it is. There is a confidence that comes with trusting in change. Change is a true gift in many ways, because it forces us to change and be a better version of ourselves than what we were before. We often can't see our faults when we are stuck in the comfort of our predictable lives. It is only when something shakes and shifts us that we then recognize that things maybe weren't working.

BALANCING YOUR FINANCES

The same rules of life balance apply to your financial life: if something is unevenly weighed down, you aren't going to be happy. So, if you are hunkering down and trying to get out of debt paying all of your bills and putting money aside, but then never allowing yourself the occasional luxury of a meal out or buying a new outfit, you aren't going to be happy. And if you are spending your money on electronics, things for the home, and lavish entertainment, but you are struggling to pay your bills and living paycheque to paycheque, you aren't going to be happy. You have to carefully balance your financial life in a way that allows you to meet all of your financial needs. It is possible to do so by focusing on your budget and building the things into it that are important to you. For example, if you want to attend a weekly boxing class and have one meal out per week with your family, then build that into your monthly budget. Make sure, however, that you add on the "extras" after you have accounted for your bill payments and put aside some for savings. You don't want to put yourself in a position where your bills are paid, and you have the extra little luxuries but no emergency fund. Unexpected things can and will happen in life, and we have to have access to money for when they do. Your car could break down, your roof may leak, or a major appliance in your home may stop working. These are not uncommon things, so it makes sense to have a plan for emergency expenses.

There are a few things that can help you tremendously balance your finances effectively:

- **Bundle services**
  Wherever possible, bundle services together so that you can pay one bill as opposed to three. For example, many companies offer Internet, TV, and phone as a bundled service. They will often give you a good discount for bundling, and it is easier to pay one bill instead of three.

- **Use cash**
  Having good old cash on you is a useful way to keep a tab on what you're spending. Withdraw money from the bank machine and use it for discretionary spending. This way, you stick to your budget and don't start dipping into money that is for other things. Some people like to use the envelope method to put money aside for things that are budgeted and can be paid in cash; that way, it is taken out and kept aside, so you don't have to worry about spending it.

- **Resist the contract**
  There are so many services, subscriptions, and businesses that want to get us on a monthly contract. This is in their best interest, but not in ours. You can't predict what life is going to look like in a few months from now. Pay for services in advance, but don't get caught up

in monthly contracts for things that you can pay for up front. Gym memberships and personal trainers are the absolute worst for this. You can find a personal trainer in your city, pay them up front, and then have no monthly fees and no gym fees. You can start running or exercising at home. Think before you sign a contract that requires a monthly financial commitment.

- **Plan big expenses**
  If you need to make a big-ticket item purchase at a furniture or appliance store, plan for it and save for it. Set aside some money from each paycheque to pay for the item. Try to plan your purchases in advance so that you aren't in a position of desperation or emergency. You want to buy a new fridge or stove before the old one breaks down, so that you can plan for it and save. Plan to get a new couch six months before you actually get it in the home to allow time to save for it.

- **Consolidate**
  Just the way bundling your phone, Internet, and television services saves you time, money, and agony, so, too, does consolidating your payments. Seek a personal loan or a line of credit to pay off all of your credit card debts and other high-interest loans. This will free up some money paid in interest and give you more cash flow, while saving you time and freeing up space on your credit cards for emergencies.

Balance isn't a difficult thing to find in life, whether it is in your everyday life or your cheque book. You simply have to be willing to observe what isn't working in your life and have the courage to admit it to yourself. So, what if you're overspending, not spending enough time with your family, or eating poorly? You can change. That was you yesterday, but that doesn't have to be you tomorrow. You can choose a different path and try something else. We cannot continue to do the same things over and over again and expect different results. It just doesn't work. So, if something isn't working in your life, change it. Balance is restored when things that used to make you feel bad no longer do, or when poor choices become life lessons. People can change. That is one of the beautiful things about being a human being. Find your balance by knowing first what is out of balance, and then change your life.

JOE ON BALANCE

When I look back over the years at people I've met and worked with, the number one issue I have consistently noticed that has caused imbalances in life is cash flow. When I say cash flow, I am specifically speaking about cash flow that does not align with financial and personal goals. Either there's too much spending happening, not enough income, or no concrete plan in place to save for goals.

There was one couple I worked with many years ago that fell into the latter category. They were so busy paying things off, they weren't having fun. They both made above average income and came to me for advice about managing their money. The income in their situation wasn't a problem — they had lots coming in. But the allocation of their money was causing all sorts of issues for them. They were living paycheque to paycheque, and sometimes drawing on cash advances through their credit cards just to meet their monthly expenses, which were astronomical.

Their mortgage payments were unusually high because of a low amortization and a personal goal they had set for themselves to pay off their mortgage within seven years. They also had car payments, which had an amortization of two years. In addition to that, they had approximately $30,000 in credit card debt and an unsecured loan for another $30,000 being paid off over two years.

The first thing I asked them was, "What are your personal goals for the next five years?" I made them write their goals down, and when we reviewed them together, it became obvious that their plan didn't meet their cash flow. I referred them to our lifestyle analysis tool (budget). Once I went over the monthly requirements and what they wanted to achieve over the next five years, they needed to make some radical changes.

This young couple came from humble beginnings. Both had parents who instilled financial advice telling them to pay off their mortgage as quickly as possible. But they wanted to travel and enjoy life before raising a family. They also wanted to save for a rainy day, and feel good about where they live. They wanted to spend money on their property by making improvements to increase their enjoyment of their home, as well as its value. This couple shared with me their vision for the life that they wanted, but they just did not know how to get there, even with the high incomes that they both had. They were too focused on paying down debt, leaving other parts of their lives neglected. I simply showed them a simple option to increase their monthly cash flow and change their financial plan to meet living life today while still saving a little bit for tomorrow. I helped show them how they could consolidate all their debts into one and concentrate on one monthly payment. They just needed to recalibrate and balance out their plans. They were so focused on getting things paid down that they weren't actually able to do any of the things they wanted to enjoy in life and were suffering unnecessarily.

Once the couple balanced things out, took my consolidation advice, and paid attention to their life goals, they ended up paying off their mortgage and doing all of the things they wanted to do. They now have two beautiful children and still invest with us to this day.

I have had to rebalance my life several times over the years. As humans, it just happens. Things become out of balance when we aren't taking care of our health, we work too much, or we aren't spending enough time with our family. The key is to acknowledge what is out of balance, and work on rebalancing all areas of your life so that you can create harmony. From that harmony will come abundance.

Finding balance and keeping it is life's work.

NOW WHAT

Now that you have read the book, and know the Financial Wellness Factors, what do you do now? How can you apply what you learned reading this book to your life?

It doesn't matter where you think you are financially. You could be in a relationship or just starting over in a new relationship, physically recovering from a major health issue or dealing with the loss of a job. The key is to start strategizing and focusing. Start your journey with the lifestyle assessment tool budget plan in Chapter 1. That is the foundation of getting your financial house in order. Without that insight and knowledge into where your money goes every month and how much you're spending, you won't be able to get on top of it or manage your money effectively. So, without a doubt, when you're finished reading this book, you absolutely should begin this work of identifying your monthly incoming vs outgoing by using the lifestyle assessment budgeting tool.

Understanding your expenses and income is the most important step in your goal to achieve financial wellness and reduce financial stress in your life. Identify things that you can control within your existing expenses. First, you will need to understand what you are spending on your fixed expenses: things like rent, a car payment, or your mortgage payment. You might also have a student debt, consolidation loan, or a line of credit. These are some examples of things that you may be able to consolidate or control by not spending at all. Income streams into your bank account can also be controlled.

If you recently just lost your job, and you are thinking, *How can I control my income?*, there is always a way. Maybe you look at selling your house and downsizing, or if you are renting, look at renting some of the portion of your home to create additional income streams. With our current market, we see a renters' market. Exploring ideas to create more income streams is very important, as well as ensuring the longevity of these income streams. Before attempting any new venture, review Chapter 3, on relationships, where we discuss mentors. We speak about different people whose success we have mimicked or followed by repeating their steps in their financial journey. Who is that mentor in your life? Set up a meeting and sit down and talk to them. Explain to them what strategies you are considering. Get them to analyze your situation and gameplan, and ask for their input. Different mentors can provide you with different opinions and perspectives, they will each have unique values that matter most to them. Remember advice from any mentor – even from us in this book – is just an opinion, and you have to ultimately decide what works best for you in your life, with your unique situation.

There was a client who needed a loan to start a side venture back in the day. At the time, he was married with three kids and renting. This client was also a friend. He had a great job and strong income, but no savings. He was trying to set up this side venture to create additional revenue. He was a computer specialist/IT guy and had begun exploring cryptocurrency. Keep in mind this was at least a decade or more before crypto really started taking off. With the loan, he would have purchased 76,000 Bitcoin. One of the reasons he wanted to venture into crypto was so that he could save a down payment to purchase a home for his family. We approved the loan, but advised him to use the loan to get the house rather than buy the Bitcoin. He was able to balance his risk, buy a home, and slowly invest in a risky asset over time while still creating security for his family. So, his home purchase didn't rely on the price of Bitcoin, and he still managed to amass wealth and security.

As we spoke about in Chapter 5, keeping balance in life is the most important factor in your overall financial well-being. Fast forward to today, that same client remains happily married, living on the outskirts of the city with his three children, and has a home worth over $1M that he can feel good about. He likely still has some crypto holdings and digital assets because he was interested in it personally. But he now has a ton of equity in his home, which is almost paid off.

We strongly believe that the answer to wealth creation is embracing and understanding the Financial Wellness Factors- Cash Flow, Attitude,

Relationships, Health, and Balance! Take stock of how you're doing in each of these areas. How is your cash flow? Do you know what you have coming and going out each month? Are you saving? Check in with your partner to make sure that your financial goals are still aligned. Then assess your attitude about finances. Do the exercise found in the "Balance" chapter to assess your feelings in the areas of income, bills, money management, potential for wealth and success. Are there any areas where you need to shift your attitude? Notice where you have negative or flawed thinking. That will get in your way. Take stock of the relationships in your life. Are you paying enough attention to your marriage? Your children? Do you have a vibrant social life? Or do you not make enough time for friends? Relationships are so important to our mental well-being and happiness. and provide us with a sense of connection and support. How is your health? Are you exercising? Sleeping properly? Eating healthy? It doesn't matter how much money you have. You could have Warren Buffet wealth, but if you aren't healthy, none of it will matter, because you will be at risk for illness or early death. Don't put yourself in that situation. Life is beautiful. Enjoy it. All of these factors must be balanced equally to lay the foundation for your financial wellness. Once you achieve balance, you will know that you are in a place of abundance, and you will easily attract success and opportunity in life.

Hopefully, this gives you a sense of what to do next. The sooner you begin getting these balls in motion, the sooner you will be able to enjoy the fruits of your labour. Life is all about the experience and magic of the journey, but if you're too stressed out, you'll miss all of that and won't be able to see the moments that mean the most in life.

Our sincerest hope is for you to receive the advice and information in this book and be able to put it into action in a tangible way that improves your health, wealth, and life as a whole. If this book helped you, please reach out to us and let us know!

AFTERWORD

Thank you for reading *Financial Wellness Factors*. This book is truly the culmination of our life's work. We couldn't have put this book together without having faced one of the scariest moments in our entire lives. Facing the possibility of our sons losing their father in 2012 really forced us to think about what we wanted to leave them with in the wake of such a tragedy. We've always been such a close and communicative family, and we wanted this book to be a guide for life of sorts for them to have, and a reference to help them navigate through life with the best advice we knew how to give them. We've always been open about business and money at the dinner table and the boys have grown up hearing us talk about this stuff, but it was important to capture it in a way that made it timeless. We thank God every single day that we are both healthy and can continue to be there for our sons today, who now work with us. One thing we've learned over the years is to never take a single day for granted.

While we wrote this book originally in 2012, we feel even stronger in our conviction today, in 2022, about what this book means and how it will impact people, given that we have just been through and are still dealing with arguably one of the most catastrophic events in our economic history. The COVID-19 pandemic affected every single country, shut down businesses and caused job losses, housing markets to soar, mental health to suffer, and now, rising inflation.

During the pandemic, there were multiple factors that contributed to the irrational housing market we all saw. Prices were skyrocketing due to interest rates that were at an all-time low, which created increased demand fuelling the feeding frenzy for buyers and causing most houses to sell for way more than what they should have, even in markets with traditionally lower-cost homes. Remote work also made people look outside of the geographical areas that they would normally want to live, which made houses in small towns suddenly skyrocket.

Working with homebuyers during this time period was difficult, because they were experiencing so much anxiety. Going in firm over asking price without selling their own homes was extremely risky, and they all wanted reassurance that their financing would be approved. The two of us worked very closely with clients during this time, with clients even calling us on weekends or after hours so that we could discuss their unique situations. We had to put a lot more time in because buyers were becoming emotional, bidding, and losing home after home – and feeling hopeless and worried sick. Many of our clients in this situation wanted to go over the purchase price that we had initially approved for them. In some cases, there were options to go higher but the rate was higher, so while we could get a loan approved, it would have been a struggle for them to afford the payments.

We had to navigate this unique time period in our business very carefully. The time we put in with clients became about so much more than simply their mortgage loans. We relied on the advice contained in this book to guide our clients through the incredible stressful market conditions and resulting hopelessness they felt. If they were worrying sick and becoming overly emotional, we'd ask them about their health and what they were doing to take care of their well-being. When couples appeared to be on different pages, we'd advise them to reconnect, do things together as a couple, and focus on creating joy so they could feel united again. We'd recommend they focus on their communication so the stress of the situation didn't take a toll on their relationship and health of their union. If a client was trying to increase their loan amount but we didn't think it was a good idea, we'd refer them to our lifestyle tool (budget planner) and get them to take a close look at their cash flow until they came to the same realization that we already knew: that it was too risky to take on more debt. We led many young couples through important conversations about cash flow, as one of the areas that causes the most conflict in a relationship.

During the pandemic, cash flow stress increased as the desperation to find and buy a home with soaring prices made people irrational and more open to risk than they would typically be – a dangerous combination. At a time when everyone was on Zoom and video conferencing, we encouraged people to come and see us in person (safely, of course) because what was happening in the market was unheard of, and people really needed support. It's difficult to emotionally connect with someone over the phone or via video chat the same way you can when they are sitting in front of you. So much of that intimacy is lost over the phone or a computer. We have always been big believers in face-to-face interaction wherever possible, and it's one of the reasons why we feel so connected to our clients and tend to stay with them throughout their lives.

Two years into the global COVID-19 pandemic, we both felt, after reviewing the book and its contents again, that our advice — even in the face of a global pandemic, rising inflation, and economic uncertainty — still remained solid. Every single factor in this book is as relevant today as it was in 2012, when we first wrote the book. In fact, it may be even more important today because of the current economic climate.

There is always going to be an element of the unknown in life. We have lived that and continue to be prepared for the unexpected the best we can. None of us can prevent pain, tragedy, or uncertainty in our lives. And without those things, the moments of joy don't have as much meaning anyway. But we can certainly prepare and safeguard our lives to better handle events when they do occur.

Some of the most stressful life events are very much tied to our financial health. If a family member falls ill and can no longer work, that results in a loss of income. If there's a divorce and a couple must start over, that can cause one or both people to face great financial hardship going from two incomes to one income. A young mom who stayed home with her kids for a few years may suddenly find herself having to find a job. A relationship loss can also represent a learning curve with how to manage money if one person handled the finances in the relationship. When our parents become elderly, sometimes it involves renovating our homes, moving them in with us, or finding them a care home. This can be a huge financial stress. Sometimes, caring for a parent means leaving a job or reducing income or hours. If a member of our family passes away, we have kids going to university, we move to a new country or province, or we decide to change our career, these things are major life events that can become a reality in our lives and impact our financial well-being. With a healthy balanced life, and sound financial planning, we are in a much better position to overcome adversity when it appears in our lives.

We sincerely hope that you've gained a glimpse into our lives and embrace the intimacy and meaning of the words contained in this book. We hope this book will help guide you on your life's journey, as we hope it will with our sons, through all of the ups and down, joys and sorrows, and the immeasurable beauty that life has to offer.

Gina & Joe

ABOUT THE AUTHORS

Husband and wife author team Gina Colalillo and Joe Trombetta have more than 2 decades of experience in the banking and lending business, including a strong mortgage enterprise that is now a family affair, with their three sons each taking on various aspects of the family business and mortgage portfolio. Titan Mortgage Group was established in 2005 in Stoney Creek, Ontario. Hard work, a positive mindset, building strong relationships with lenders, clients, and investors have been the building blocks to Titan's success. The Trombetta's have become established in the Hamilton Stoney Creek community supporting many local events and charities and using their financial expertise to help and guide others.

GINA COLALILLO

Gina has helped generations of families make the biggest purchase decision of their lives. Making strong meaningful connections and building incredible relationships is what Gina does best. Gina is known for her caring nature and professional attitude and has helped every client that has walked through the doors at Titan Mortgage for the past 20 years. A dedication and commitment to the mortgage industry has been paramount to Gina's career success. Gina is an experienced mortgage broker with multiple degrees in both business and education under her belt. Gina places a huge priority on transparency, ethics and advocating for clients by helping to simplify and demystify the mortgage experience for her clients. She obtains financing that is suitable to each client's unique situation and makes even the impossible possible. Gina prioritizes work life balance in her own life and ensures that her family and health take priority. The first 16 years of Gina's career was spent working for large corporations and teaching, which have become important to Gina's career again as she enjoys mentoring clients on financial wellbeing and life balance. Writing this book with Joe was a big part of that.

JOSEPH TROMBETTA

Joe has extensive experience in the mortgage industry and a deep understanding and passion for financing and lending. With over 30 years in the mortgage business, Joe's experience extends to banks, trust companies and mortgage companies as well as development projects. Joe has enhanced his experience with his dedication to continuing education and his constant drive to challenge himself. Joe's vast experience with a variety of lending institutions and client scenarios have given him deep industry insight into gaps that exist, while enabling him to build his own practice to offer a better client experience. The trigger that convinced Joe to start his own practice was simple: while working at larger institutions, he was unable to help everyone who walked through his door. That didn't sit right with Joe. Now thanks to his own practice he can proudly offer solutions to each and every customer who walks through the door, providing clients with all of their mortgage needs in one place, and with a personal touch.

Having built the framework for Titan's success, Joe expanded his reach into mortgage investments, and now owns and manages (along with his sons) over 300 properties/units with Village Creek Living. Joe loves mentoring others and helping his community!

ACKNOWLEDGMENTS

Writing this book has really brought to the forefront how grateful we both are for our blessed lives. The reason we embarked on this project in the first place was because we were uncertain about our family's future together, and whether our sons would have their father around to pass on this important life knowledge. It was a legacy that was important to us. And we knew if it was important enough to share with our sons, then it was certainly important enough to share with others.

We are thankful every single day to God for granting us the good health that we both possess to continue our work together at our company with our family and our colleagues. Without good health not much else matters. It is why we strive daily to ensure that our lives include a strong focus on eating well, regular exercise, stress reduction, and positive relationships. When you've been through a serious illness, and the untimely death of a family member, you truly feel more grateful for each and every day you have to spend here on earth with those you love.

Our sons inspired the content of this book and we want to acknowledge and thank our forever angel Nicholas, and Daniel, Thomas and Matthew for being such incredible young men and for wanting to be a part of what we've built. We are very much in awe of how our sons have grown into the professionals that they are today. It is such a delight to work alongside them each and every day and to watch them become successful in their own right. We are blessed to have such a close family.

We would also like to thank our parents for instilling in us the value and meaning of a dollar. As immigrants they didn't come to this country with very much. And because of their work ethic and commitment to saving for the future, we owe our success to them and continue to honour the family legacies that they built.

We'd be remiss without mentioning our incredible staff at Titan Mortgage Group. It feels strange even saying "staff" because we are truly like family. We share in each other's joys, support each other during the lows, and rally when things need to get done. Lisa, Cristina, Donna, Rita, Jerry and Antonio have been by our side for many years and are the backbone of our business.

Thank you for being such beautiful human beings and for making work a joy to come to every day.

left to right, Gina, Lisa, Cristina, Rita, Donna (The Titan Ladies, 2018)

Thank you so much to Charlie for always having our back as a friend and for really jumping in and helping us push this book project forward. And to Selina for helping us realize our vision and making it all make sense. We couldn't have done it without you. And to our colleagues and professional network; all of the incredible people who we've been lucky to build meaningful relationships with over the years. Thank you for your support.

A huge thank you to our friends and extended family, with whom we've shared so many special moments as we were writing this book. Thank you for listening, contributing, and lending your support to us throughout the years. We are blessed to have you in our lives.

We want to acknowledge and thank our clients, who often stay in our lives. We have befriended so many clients over the years and have shared in their successes, far beyond their mortgages. Without you, we would have never been able to build the business that we have today, and we will forever be grateful.

And finally to you, the reader; thank you for being here, for reading our book and allowing us to be a part of your life. We sincerely hope that this book has a positive impact on your life in some way. And we'd love to hear from you if it does, so please don't be shy!

God Bless.

Financial Wellness
Factors Meeting

Printed in Canada